Most business letters c̶...
letters—yes, even those dealing with collection and refusal of credit. It is the spirit, not the subject matter, that
counts.

FIRST IMPRESSIONS

When you meet someone who has a safety pin replacing a button on his shirt or someone who hasn't bothered to remove her chipped and worn fingernail polish,
you receive an important first impression image of this
person. Similarly, correspondence that precedes us is an
introduction to who we are and makes an initial impression on the recipient.

ATTENTION TO DETAIL

Executive secretaries are expert in judging the mail; a
communication arriving in a cheap envelope, perhaps
addressed in poor form, will prejudice him or her
against it. Therefore, treat first things first; choose paper
and envelope with care.

Books available from
the HarperPaperbacks Reference Library

LETTERS FOR ALL OCCASIONS

Revised Edition

ALFRED STUART MYERS

Edited by Lynn Ferrari

📕 HarperPaperbacks
A Division of HarperCollinsPublishers

HarperPaperbacks *A Division of* HarperCollins*Publishers*
10 East 53rd Street, New York, N.Y. 10022

A trade paperback of this book was published in 1993
by HarperCollins*Publishers.*

Cover photograph by Karen Capucilli

First HarperPaperbacks printing: July 1994

Printed in the United States of America

HarperPaperbacks and colophon are trademarks of
HarperCollins*Publishers*

10 9 8 7 6 5 4

CONTENTS

Part Two

TYPES OF SOCIAL LETTERS

Part Three

TYPES OF BUSINESS LETTERS

FOREWORD

Think about letters you have received and how many of them, business or personal, have left you unmoved, unmotivated, and uninspired.

Perhaps you didn't even consciously realize exactly why you failed to react favorably. You just put the letter aside and gave it not another thought.

The lack may have been the result of the physical makeup of the letter; or of the words used to express an idea; or of the general tone and "spirit." It could be that all these factors were involved.

If you did consciously react to a letter that left you unmoved, you may have wondered, "Do I write letters like that? Do my letters really say what I want them to say? Is the impression actually what I want it to be?" Your answers may all be favorable to your own letter-writing efforts, but the process of periodically reflecting on what we do is usually helpful and certainly is a case where a bad example can be a good example. It sometimes pays to analyze a poorly written letter, when you get one, and to discover its real failings—then to be sure to avoid them in your own letter writing.

How we represent ourselves on paper is often the first impression someone else has of us—a job query, a note to a son's or daughter's future in-laws, a letter of introduction to a prospective client—each can be the way someone else initially "meets" us.

Our letters also can cause another to be more favorably inclined to hear our point of view, or remember us with fondness. A well-written complaint about inconsiderate treatment is taken more seriously than a wild and accusing one that sounds and looks as though it is written by a crank. A beautifully crafted thank you for whatever reason makes the recipient doubly glad he or she entertained you, gave you a gift, or performed an act of kindness in the first place.

The other part of a letter to which we react is the way it looks. Certainly you would not keep a business appointment wearing old jeans and a torn T-shirt or engage in an interview without careful consideration of the good impression you want to make. With letters, it is equally important to create an effective, favorable impression, for whatever purpose the letter may be written. To that end, there are certain fundamental principles to be applied. They are simple, but, at all times, they should be strictly observed.

The purpose here is to explain these fundamental principles in a straightforward, nontechnical fashion and to give examples that will illustrate them and show how to impart that "spirit" behind the good letter, mentioned earlier. This book is intended to provide a simple, practical guide for the reader who wishes to master the art of effective social and business correspondence.

Part One

THE FORM AND FORMALITY
OF EFFECTIVE LETTERS

SOCIAL LETTERS

When you meet someone who has a safety pin replacing a button on his shirt or who hasn't bothered to remove her chipped and worn fingernail polish, you receive a first impression image of this person. In the same way, correspondence that precedes us is an introduction to who we are and makes an initial impression on the recipient. The appearance and legibility of the letter and the choice of paper and envelope produce the first impression, favorable or unfavorable, that carries over into the letter itself, for good or ill. This may seem obvious, but it is surprising how many people are careless in these respects and forfeit an important advantage they might have gained at the start.

HANDWRITTEN LETTERS

Most social correspondence, whether a letter to a friend, an informal invitation, or a thank-you or condolence note, is written by hand. This is particularly true with the latter two—a note received in your own handwriting seems to convey your feelings much more personally than one that is written on a word processor or typewriter.

Remember that having to struggle to decipher handwriting detracts from the content of the letter—make the effort to write neatly and clearly.

MECHANICALLY PRODUCED LETTERS

It used to be that personal letters were never written by typewriter, probably because a typewritten communication was reserved for and associated with business correspondence. Letters today are more frequently typed or word-processed, and there is nothing unfriendly or incorrect about using this form.

One advantage of word processing for frequent letter writers is the ability to save the letter you have written. It will become a reference for future letters, in order to refresh your memory about previous correspondence.

Personal notes, as discussed earlier, should still be handwritten. When a handicapping condition exists, or when handwriting is truly illegible, these notes may be typed or word-processed, although the signature should be handwritten, if at all possible. Although the form and formality of any correspondence contributes to the pleasure or annoyance of the recipient, the content is the point of communication in the first place. If a letter can't be read, there is no communication!

PAPER

Letter paper should, above all else, be tasteful. Too-bright colors and busy designs make letters difficult to read. White, ivory, light blue, and gray paper is always correct, as are thin-ruled borders in complementary colors.

Neatness of appearance is enhanced by even margins, at both left and right—a slight margin on the right, a little broader one on the left. The letter should be neatly folded so that the edges, top, and bottom meet evenly, and so that the first page faces the person who opens the envelope and unfolds the letter.

Envelopes should be the correct size for the stationery and should match the color of the stationery.

PAGING

Stationery

Sparing trees is a consideration in whether to write on the back of single-sheet stationery, but so is legibility. If the paper is thin and writing shows through, then it is best not to write on both sides. If the paper is heavy enough to prevent show-through, then by all means write on the back, being sure to number the pages after page one.

Folded Stationery

Stationery that is $8^1/_2'' \times 11''$ or $8^1/_2'' \times 14''$ flat is sometimes sold folded, end to end, with a border, engraving, or another design on the front. There is considerable variety in the ways you may select a pagination sequence:

1. Write on pages one and three up and down, and on pages two and four sideways.
2. Write on pages one and four up and down, and on pages two and three (the inside pages) sideways, using them as one long page.
3. Write on all four pages up and down, in regular sequence—one, two, three, four. This is perhaps best for the reader, who can then find and read the pages of your letter as she or he would read those of a book, easily and quickly.

A three-page letter may be written on pages one and three up and down, and on page two sideways; or it may be written on pages one, two, and three up and down.

A two-page note may be written on pages one and four up and down, with the two inside pages left blank; or it may be written on pages one and three up and down.

Whichever of these procedures you use, again—number your pages.

Foldover Notes

Foldover notepaper is generally used for thank-you notes, notes of condolence, invitations, and other short messages. Its form is a piece of paper folded in half twice to an approximate size of no less than 3″ × 5.″

The note may begin on the front if the paper is plain or has a design element or monogram in the upper left corner. If the note is short, it is continued on the inside, bottom half, and concluded, if necessary, on the back. If the note is long, page two may begin on the top half of the inside and continue as a single page to the bottom, concluding, if necessary, on the back.

If the front has a centered design, then the note begins on the inside bottom half, continues on the back, and concludes, if necessary, on the inside top half. It never begins on the top half of the inside.

Informals are actually a more formal form of foldover notepaper that has the name of an individual or a couple, including titles (Mrs. Charles Northshield or Mr. and Mrs. Charles Northshield), engraved or printed on the center front. They are almost always white or ivory.

PERSONALIZATION

Personal stationery may be further personalized by the addition of the sender's name and address, initials, or family crest. On letter paper, these elements are generally centered at the top of the paper. On foldover notepaper and informals, a full name is centered on the front while initial monograms or crests are either centered or placed in the upper left corner.

Embossing

Initials—with the first letter of the last name in the center, the first letter of the first name to the left, and the first letter of the middle or maiden name, if the paper is for a married woman who has taken her husband's last name, to the right—may be engraved, printed, or embossed.

Full names and addresses may be embossed on the letter paper as well as on the envelope, although embossing is sometimes difficult to see or read and is not the form preferred by the United States Post Office for return addresses.

The embossing process uses no ink but rather raises the letters so they are visible on the paper.

Engraving

Full names or initial monograms may be engraved on stationery as well as on the envelope flap. Engraving, which is fairly expensive, produces raised, inked letters, usually in a complementary color to the paper (dark blue on light blue paper, for example, or dark blue, black, or dark brown on cream or ivory). Other less expensive processes, such as offset printing, do not produce raised letters but otherwise can be just as elegant. Titles usually are not used on full-sized stationery—the name may be printed "Elizabeth Northshield" instead of "Mrs. Charles Northshield." Men seldom use the title "Mr." preceding their names. The address and sometimes the telephone number are centered below the name. The title (Mr., Miss, Ms., Mrs.) often is included on the envelope flap.

Family Crests

A coat of arms is not frequently seen today, but may be engraved on personal stationery if a family has used it, or a family crest, through the years. As it was at the time of its medieval origin, the use of a crest is reserved exclusively for male members of a family or for a married couple. This heraldic rule precludes women from using their husband's family crest on individual, personal stationery. Unmarried women may use their father's coat of arms on a lozenge, a diamond-shaped device, without the crest or motto.

FORM

Both typed or word-processed and handwritten letters follow the same format described next in this chapter, with the following particulars specific to them:

- Single spacing is ordinarily preferable to double spacing.
- The body of the letter is begun two spaces below the salutation when mechanically produced, and the equivalent of two spaces when handwritten.
- New paragraphs should be indented five spaces.
- The body of the letter should have at least one inch margins, more if the letter is short.

The Heading

The heading, which is one of the standard parts of a letter, is at the upper right-hand side and includes your address and the date. It should not be jammed against the very top of the paper. An upper margin of at least one inch and a right-hand margin of about three-quarters of an inch should be allowed. This means that you must start your address, if in handwriting, well toward the middle of the top of the page. If your address is already engraved or printed on the stationery, then just the date is placed at the upper right-hand side.

It is courteous to include your address, even in a letter to your best friend, so that he or she doesn't have to look it up when responding to your letter, or in case it has been lost or misplaced. The date gives a reference to when you wrote and to the events about which you write, in case the recipient wishes to refresh his or her memory and/or does not write back to you immediately.

THE MONTH AND THE YEAR

The name of the month should be spelled out in full: October, February, etc.; and the year also should be written in full: 1994, not '94. An abbreviation is all right in memoranda, but not in correspondence. Except in very formal letters, do not use the ordinal numbers or an abbreviation of them (first, second, 1st, 2nd). Write, for example, April 5, July 2.

THE ADDRESS

Names of cities, even if long, should be spelled in full, but names of states may be abbreviated. Since it is not easy to remember the correct abbreviation, the principal approved, shortened forms are listed on page 66 for quick reference.

It is best, in the body of the letter, to spell in full the words Road, Boulevard, Square, Building, Place, Avenue, and Street, although the rules for envelopes are different and are discussed on page 64. The following is a correct form of heading:

> 90 Hillside Avenue
> St. James, NY 11780
> October 2, 1993

The Inside Address

The inside address consists of the name and address of the person to whom you are writing. It is customary in business correspondence but is not generally used in a letter to a friend.

Its use is proper, however, in some letters requiring a touch of formality; for example, in a letter of appreciation you might write to a speaker or performer who had appeared at your club, or in a letter to a prominent person whose opinion on an issue or event you wish to obtain. The inside address may also be used in a letter from one member of an organization to another that is personal but at the same time includes semi-business questions or information.

This component of a letter begins with the recipient's name and appears at the left margin, six spaces below the date in the return address, and two spaces above the salutation:

> 1715 South Camden Avenue
> Los Angeles, CA 90025
> March 24, 1994

Miss Esther Julia Coleman
253 East Delaware Place
Chicago, IL 60611

Dear Esther,

The Salutation

A salutation, as the term implies, is your opening greeting to the person to whom you are writing. You use it just as you would address a person formally or informally, face to face, before you enter into conversation with him. Further, as in that case, so in correspondence, the degree of formality will differ according to how well you know the person. In correspondence you should maintain a degree of formality with all except those whom you know very well.

In informal correspondence, you should use, in the salutation, the same name that you use in talking with the person. If the letter is to a close friend and you know him or her by a nickname, you would use that: "Dear Susie," instead of "Dear Susan;" "Dear Bob," not "Dear Robert." You would write, in the same manner, "Dear Grandma" and "Dear Aunt Ruth"—anything more formal would be ridiculous since these are the names you use when you chat with them.

Although extremely personal letter content is never a good idea, a very intimate form of greeting may be used, such as "Dearest One," or "My very own Darling," or any other endearing title.

The salutation is two spaces below the inside address in a typewritten or word-processed letter, and about one-half inch below the inside address in a handwritten letter. In social correspondence, the salutation ends with a comma.

The Body of the Letter

This is the main content of the letter—the "meat." It constitutes the whole purpose or object of the correspondence. Remember this from beginning to end, all the time you are writing, and make your letter clear and direct. Let it express sincerity throughout, whatever its particular subject or purpose: to offer an invitation, to express sympathy, to congratulate someone on a special occasion, or just to "chat" with a friend and give him all the latest news.

THE USE OF "I"

There used to be a hard-and-fast rule, "Never begin a letter or a paragraph with the pronoun 'I,'" just as there was a similarly hard-and-fast rule, "Never end a sentence with a preposition." These rules have been relaxed because they seemed too arbitrary and artificial. A letter in which you strictly avoid ever beginning a paragraph with the first-person pronoun is apt to become a rather stilted affair—especially if it is a letter to a friend or acquaintance.

Nevertheless, it is not good taste to use the pronoun "I" a great deal in any letter, either social or business. In conversation, you do not enjoy listening to a person whose principal pronoun is "I". Nor do you enjoy a letter in which the "I" overweighs everything else. Remember that as you write your letters. Of course, in letters to friends of long standing you do not need to be too particular on this point, but even in such correspon-

dence it is good taste to avoid undue repetition of the
first-person singular pronoun.

CLARITY

"Put yourself in the other person's place," is a common bit of excellent advice too seldom followed. It is
particularly helpful in letter writing. If you heed this
advice, you will make yourself entirely clear; you will
say all that you mean to say, and, just as important, you
will not say what you did not mean to say. You will not
leave your reader to guess your meaning, or to try to
"read between the lines." Moreover, you will express
yourself in an interesting manner; you will not repeat
yourself—a very boring habit with too many writers, as
well as speakers. You will avoid hackneyed expressions,
worn threadbare from excessive use, such as, "It's such
a small world," "Two heads are better than one," "I
don't know much about art, but I know what I like,"
"He's a chip off the old block," "Once bitten, twice
shy." Such bromides are godsends for people who do
not want to make the mental effort required to express
an idea with some degree of originality.

If you put yourself in the other person's place, you
will also make your letter "mechanically" and visually
neat; clearly legible, not crowded, free of smudges and
of words substituted for words crossed out. Whether
handwritten, typewritten, or word-processed, only the
most informal letters may have insertions above the lines
—words or phrases you originally omitted.

VALUE OF SELF-CRITICISM

Some of the points just emphasized may seem trivial. They are not. It is surprising how many letter writers make a bad impression because they fail to give enough attention to some or all of these things. One of the best safeguards is to give a special reading to your letter before you seal it and send it beyond your recall. It is at this time, especially, that you should put yourself in the reader's place. Sit back, at leisure, and read it as if someone else had written it and sent it to you. What would you think of it? If honestly applied, that is about as good a test as there is. Make use of it regularly and sincerely, and you will find that self-criticism can be truly valuable.

The trouble with a great deal of self-criticism is that there is too much self in it and not enough criticism. Make it honest, and you will find that it will materially help you to improve your correspondence. When you give your letter a final critical reading, criticize it on all points: the content; the expression; the "atmosphere," the layout, or mechanics. The following are questions you might ask yourself about the letter:

Is it really interesting, or just dull and routine? Have I talked about things that will interest the reader—not just about my own affairs? Have I made correct use of the English language, and have I made myself perfectly clear—not only so that I can be understood, but especially so that I cannot be misunderstood? If an invitation, have I been clear on the dates, times, formality or informality of the occasion, and all the components it includes? Is there an attractive "atmosphere" to my letter—a real personality behind it? Have I observed the funda-

mental rules of mechanics that insure an attractive and technically correct letter? Have I written legibly so that the reader will not be obliged to "translate," interpret, or just plain guess?

Ending a Letter

If you were talking with a friend or acquaintance, you would end your conversation, not just by turning and walking away or by hanging up the telephone without saying "goodbye," but with some polite or friendly farewell. In the same way, letters should end gracefully, with a closing word of good wishes.

Following your farewell in the body of the letter, skip the equivalent of two spaces and write a complimentary close. The formality or informality of this closing statement depends on that of the letter and the degree of acquaintance with the person to whom you are writing.

Very Formal: *Respectfully yours, Yours respectfully, Faithfully yours, Very truly yours, Yours truly.*

Less Formal: *Cordially, Cordially yours, Sincerely, Sincerely yours, Yours very sincerely, Always sincerely yours, As ever, Ever yours, Always yours.* You will note that, among these, there is a varying degree of informality. Naturally you will make your choice according to how well you know the person to whom you are writing.

Entirely Informal: *With much love, Your loving son (daughter, grandson, nephew, etc.), With all my love, Affectionately, Affectionately yours.* In family letters and other intimate personal letters, of course, any terms of affection and endearment are appropriate in the complimentary close.

The complimentary close should end with a comma. Two spaces in a typewritten or word-processed letter should be left between the body of the letter and the closing. It should be placed to line up with the heading or begin approximately in the middle of the page.

The Signature

Although at first one's signature might seem to be a matter of the utmost simplicity, requiring no discussion at all, such is not the case.

POSITION

First, the signature written in the wrong position makes a poor impression. In a handwritten letter, it should begin two or three lines below the complimentary close and slightly to the right, so that it will end at or near the right-hand margin of the letter. In a mechanically produced letter, the same positioning is applicable unless your name has been typed four spaces beneath the complimentary close. In this case, your signature is centered in between those two elements.

The signature should always be handwritten in ink; ordinarily no title is attached, although in formal correspondence a doctor may add M.D. or a minister D.D., for example: *Eugene M. Wasserman*, M.D., or *Henry E. Smithson*, D.D. The full middle name is signed if the individual is accustomed to using it—otherwise not. If there are only two names, be sure to spell out the first name. Naturally, you would sign a letter to a close relative or special friend with only your first name or nickname following the closing:

> Affectionately,
> Rebecca

or

> Love,
> Mark

WOMEN'S SIGNATURES

There are still some guidelines that differentiate women's from men's signatures, generally having to do with preference and marital status. As with all correspondence, the degree of formality determines the exact form of the signature.

A single woman will sign formal correspondence with her formal signature. It may be two names—*Deirdre Jordan*; three names—*Deirdre Mary Jordan*; or first name, middle initial, and last name—*Deirdre M. Jordan*. In very informal correspondence, she will, of course, use her first name or nickname only.

A married woman's formal signature will be her full name (first, maiden, and married): *Kristin McCullough Brown*. Her maiden name may be omitted in the case of rather informal letters: *Kristin Brown*. In very informal letters, her first name, or a nickname by which she is known to close friends, will be used. If she has retained her maiden name, she would of course use that; and if she has continued to use her maiden name in business but uses her married name socially, she would use the name by which the recipient will know her—her married name for social friends, her maiden name for business associates in social correspondence. For the latter, if the correspondence is a joint social invitation from the woman and her husband to business associates who know her by her professional, or maiden, name, she would write *Kristin McCullough and Brent Brown* or *Kristin and Brent Brown*, hoping the recipients will determine who she is by the nature of the invitation. A widow continues to use her married name if that is what she used when her husband was living.

A divorced woman may legally reassume her maiden name, in which case she naturally reassumes the signature she used before her marriage. If she prefers to do so, however, after her divorce she may use the same signature she used while she was married, with one exception—she may not continue to use *Mrs. John Smith.* Rather, if she were to use the title *Mrs.,* it would be *Mrs. Mary Smith.* Rather archaic, formal reference may be made to her as *Mrs. Green Smith* (title, maiden name, married name).

LEGIBILITY

Finally, let us repeat that the signature should always be *clearly* written. When you come right down to it, you are doing your reader a discourtesy if you give him or her the task of "unscrambling" a signature that is practically illegible. After all, if you were asked what your name is, you would not mumble it behind your teeth so that it could not be heard by the person who inquired. Sign your name so that it is perfectly clear to anyone who can read. This applies whether the communication is social or business, formal or informal.

THE ENVELOPE

Clear information and proper form on an envelope are important both to the Post Office and to the recipient of your letter. With today's technological advances, as much mail as is possible is now electronically sorted and is processed faster if the envelope is addressed correctly. Correct form has changed in the last decade, and although your letter will eventually reach its destination if improperly addressed, it will reach it much more quickly if the new guidelines are followed.

To the recipient, it is much more gratifying to receive a letter which employs the correct status, title and spelling of one's name than to receive a letter addressed to Mr. when the proper abbreviation is really Dr. or to see *Jeanne Verrilli* when *Jean* is the appropriate spelling. For information about correct titles and acceptable abbreviations, see page 64.

In social correspondence, the envelope is sometimes addressed in indented form, although the Post Office requests block form for electronic scanning:

Ms. Nancy Miller
   20 Laury Drive
      Fairhaven, NJ 08801-0875

Ms. Nancy Miller
20 Laury Drive
Fairhaven, NJ 08801-0875

Whichever form you select, indented or block, you must use it both for the envelope and for the inside heading of the letter.

Also note that, when known, the use of the five-digit plus four-digit zip code speeds processing.

Return Address

Be sure to place a return address on your envelope, in the event that your letter goes astray or the addressee has moved. Postal authorities advise that the sender's address be placed in the upper left-hand corner of the envelope, on the same side as the address. (In social correspondence, however, the return address is often placed on the back flap of the envelope.) Such special notations as "Please forward" or "Personal" may be written on the front of the envelope, to the left of the recipient's name.

The return address should follow the form of the address, either indented or block, but remember that the Post Office can only electronically scan block form.

BUSINESS LETTERS

As in the case of social letters, the initial effect produced by business letters is very important. The paper and envelope introduce you, so to speak, into the office of the person to whom you write. If your letter does not make a good impression, even before it is opened, it may fail to obtain the reception you want it to have.

Executive secretaries are expert in judging the mail; a communication arriving in a cheap envelope, perhaps addressed in poor form, will prejudice him or her against it. If, when he or she opens it, the paper and the form produce a less-than-professional look, your letter may be given a place in the day's mail where it will receive a "later reading." If such a letter goes directly to the executive, the impression is apt to be even worse. Therefore, treat first things first; choose paper and envelope with care.

Attention to Details

The following points relating to the entire letter should be carefully observed. Negligence with respect to these matters often mars what would otherwise have been a job well done.

Accuracy

You should strive for accuracy not only in mechanical and technical details, but especially in references and statements, dates, titles, spelling (especially names of persons and of firms), the use of language and punctuation, and arguments. In all things be accurate. It is much better to rewrite a letter than to send it out containing dubious or incorrect material.

Thoroughness

When you read your letter over before releasing it—and you always should—make certain that you have covered all essential points. If you are writing a reply to a correspondent, be sure that your answer is comprehensive and covers any questions that he or she expressed or implied. Don't make it necessary for that person to write again for information you ought to have given in the first place.

Conciseness

Some people who believe in being concise have the mistaken idea that they must be curtly abrupt. This is far from the case. In a business letter, each sentence must be grammatically complete, and each paragraph must deal adequately with its main point. But a concise sentence, paragraph, or letter need not lack completion or courtesy. It merely omits wordiness, repetition, and nonessential "trimmings" in the form of a long, drawn-out beginning or ending. By being concise you will gain friends, not lose them.

Clarity

To write a letter that will be clear to the recipient, you must first have a definite idea of what you mean to say. If you are vague in your thought, how can you expect the reader to grasp it immediately? To be clear does not necessarily mean the use of a great many words to express an idea. It means using the right words. Read your letter over before sending it, and don't be satisfied unless and until it possesses clarity.

Promptness

If you cannot answer a letter promptly, acknowledge its receipt and state that you will give it your early attention. Include a courteous expression of thanks for the letter.

PAPER

Business paper used should be a good white bond, and generally of standard business size ($8^1/_2'' \times 11''$) with an envelope to match. The better the quality, the more effective the impression.

The matter of having paper and envelope match and fit is more than of little importance. Business offices sometimes receive letters on paper that does not match the envelope in kind and quality, and which has had to be folded in a special way to fit. It is hardly necessary to emphasize that such "misfits" are bad taste and bad business.

Company Letterhead

When stationery is used by various people in a company it carries the name of the firm, with the address, telephone number, and facsimile (fax) number, usually at the top. If the company has a logo it regularly uses, this symbol is also included on the letterhead. Personnel using this stationery would, below their typed signature, type their title if it isn't otherwise indicated on the letterhead.

Personalized Company Stationery

Many companies have stationery printed (or engraved) for their executives. The executive's name and title are usually printed in the upper left-hand or right-hand corner on the company's stationery (which includes the name of the company, logo if used, address, fax number, and the direct telephone number of the executive). In this case, the writer's title would not be repeated under his or her name following the closing.

Personal Business Notepaper

Often executives have personal office stationery in addition to personalized company stationery. The paper is printed or engraved with the executive's name and the firm's address. Titles (Mr., Ms, Mrs., Miss) are not used unless the person is a doctor or military officer using his or her title. Often, this paper is smaller in size than $8^1/2'' \times 11''$ since it is used for brief notes, usually as an attachment to documents or as notes of thanks or congratulations, reminders of appointments, and other correspondence of this type.

Paper for Personal Letters to a Business

It is frequently necessary to write personal letters to a business—a utility, the telephone company, a credit card company, etc. These letters are generally regarding business one encounters with this company as an individual (homeowner, renter, purchaser, etc.) not as a member of a company. Stationery for these kinds of letters can simply be plain white bond paper with a return address and heading used as described on page 10. They should never be written on your office stationery or letterhead, since their content has nothing to do with your company.

The exception would be if you were asked to write a letter of reference for someone, in which case, although the person may not have been in the employ of your company but known to you in another capacity, the use of your company letterhead adds credence to your stature as a reference-giver.

Memos

When communicating internally, from your department to the office of another department, for example, you would use the form of a memorandum, or memo, rather than a business letter. Some companies have stationery that is simply headed, "Memo;" others have memorandum paper with the name of the company in a single line at the top, and still others have preprinted "To/From" forms to be used for this purpose.

Memos should always be dated, include the name or names of the person(s) to whom they are directed and the name of the person by whom they are being sent, and the purpose of the memo. The body of the memo includes concise information. Text begins two spaces or more down from the heading. For example:

June 12, 1993

To: Ann Idzik

From: Betty Johnston

Re: June 5th Seminar Schedule

Plans for the new employee seminar have been finalized, as follows: (etc.).

The memo should be signed either at the end, which is the most often-used form, or initialed or signed next to the name of the sender in the heading.

Adhesive Notes

Small pads of paper with an adhesive backing in a strip along one side are handy ways to add a note to a document or correspondence you are sending to someone else. They may be imprinted with your name, but most often they are plain. The only caution for their use is that you write legibly and neatly, even if your only message is "F.Y.I." (For Your Information). If your name is not imprinted, it is best to sign the note, since there is no other indication that it is from you.

PAGING

The paging and sequence of the business letter do not permit the variation allowed in the case of social letters. If a letter exceeds one page in length, the next page is simply another sheet, in regular sequence. In proportion to the total number of business letters written, not a great many are longer than one page, since single spacing, almost universally practiced, makes it possible to include much material on one page.

A TWO-PAGE LETTER

If, however, your communication runs more than one page, you should number each succeeding page in the upper right-hand corner, placing immediately before the page number the name of the person to whom you are writing. There should be a margin of about $1/4$ to $1/2$ inch at the right of the page number, or it may line up with the right-hand margin. Placing of name and number at the top of the page is advisable in order that any pages which get scattered or misplaced may be immediately identified.

Mrs. Fran Lowy—2

Another form of identification is to include the date on the second page as well. To do this, the name is placed at the left margin, the page number is centered between two dashes, and the date is placed at the right margin.

Mrs. Fran Lowy   - 2 -   April 5, 1994

When the letter runs only a little more than one page, it is best, for the sake of appearance, that there be at least three lines on the second page in addition to the heading information. To accomplish this, simply set the heading, date, inside address, and salutation lower on the first page, and make the margins wider. This will carry over at least three lines of material to the second page.

The letter should be neatly folded twice, to make three laps, or folds, each of about equal width. Thus it will fit neatly into the long envelope commonly used for business correspondence. It is a convenience to the person opening the letter if you make the second fold so that it comes a fraction of an inch below the top of the page. This leaves an overlapping edge that can be grasped for quick and easy unfolding. To fit a large sheet into a small envelope, fold the sheet in half (horizontally) and then fold it twice from right to left.

FORM

Business letters are single spaced, with paragraphs indicated by a five-space indent, or by double spacing between paragraphs that begin flush with the left margin (no indent).

Keep in mind that a letter composed of only two or three lengthy paragraphs does not look as neat and attractive as one broken into three or four short paragraphs. Moreover, comparatively short paragraphs are more easily read and more quickly understood than long ones. The first and the last paragraphs especially should be relatively brief.

The Heading

Assuming that the business stationery already has an engraved or printed letterhead that includes the name of the company, possibly the name of the person sending the letter and his or her title, the company address, telephone number, and facsimile (fax) number, your heading consists solely of the date, at the right margin. A second form for business letters is to line all elements up at the left margin, from the date to the closing and signature.

If you are not using business stationery with imprinted information already in place, then a simple and effective heading should have the name of the firm or individual at the top center, from one to one and one-half inches below the top of the page; one space below, street address; one space farther down, city, or town, state, and zip code. Two spaces below, centered, you may place the telephone number. If you type the date in the center, place it two or three spaces lower.

Another arrangement might be to type the telephone number at the left, about two or three spaces below the heading, and the date exactly opposite, on the right. In this case, leave the same margin at the left of the telephone number and at the right of the date—from three-quarters to one inch. This arrangement will make a pleasing and well-balanced appearance in relation to the heading.

The following examples illustrate what has been described above:

                    Douglas N. Jones
                    2 Fox Run
                    Concord, NH 03301-9808

                                        October 2, 1993

Douglas N. Jones
2 Fox Run
Concord, NH 03301-9808

October 2, 1993

Douglas N. Jones
2 Fox Run
Concord, NH 03301-9808

(603) 835-4509   October 2, 1993

The Inside Address

The inside address, in its most detailed form, may consist of as many as six lines; in its simplest form, as few as two. Whether simple or complex, it should be the same in content and form as the address on the envelope, whereby the Post Office is enabled to deliver your letter to the right person at the right place.

The two-line address is sometimes sufficient when the letter is sent to a very small town where everybody is known, or to a prominent federal, state, or municipal official.

Ms. Jo Alyce Newgaard
Sky Falls, KS 66208

or

> Secretary of the Treasury
> Washington, D.C. 20510

A three-line address would include the number and street, a four-line address the individual, the company name, the number and street, and the city (town), state, and zip code.

Probably the most common is the five-line address:

> Ms. Judith Kemp
> Senior Vice President
> D. M. B. & B.
> 1675 Broadway
> New York, NY 10019

When known, the inside address should include the title of the individual. This title should immediately follow the name of the individual, provided it is not so long that it would extend far across the page and look awkward. In this case, the title would be placed on the line following the name, as illustrated above.

A six-line address could be arranged like the following example:

> Mr. Scott Dunn
> Director of Public Information
> Social Activities Group
> The Anderson Foundation
> 18 West End Avenue
> Duluth, MN 55801

We have mentioned the advisability of placing a person's title on the second line if it would unduly extend the first line. But occasionally some line other than the first will be so long that it, too, would present a poor appearance. In such a case, it is permissible to break the line and indent the second part several spaces:

> Mr. Joseph Carlucci
> Department of Construction
> and Public Works
> San Carlos, CA 94070

As with social correspondence, there are abbreviations which are acceptable in business correspondence. Please refer to page 64 for information on acceptable abbreviations.

The exact placement of the inside address is particularly important because, once made, it determines both the up-and-down spacing and the left-hand margin of the letter proper. Since you want the finished product to give a pleasing, well-balanced appearance, the inside address should be considerably lower if the letter is to be brief. Otherwise, the letter will not be centered on the page.

There is no hard-and-fast rule as to where to start the inside address—in a long letter, not less than two spaces below the level of the date line; in a short one, considerably farther down than that, so that a proper bottom margin may remain at the end of the letter. The left-hand margin, like the vertical placement of the inside address, may vary according to the length of the letter. Even in a long letter, the left-hand margin should not be less than one inch; it may be slightly more.

In a very brief letter, the margins may be considerably more than one inch if necessary to maintain the proper appearance for your correspondence.

The regular position for the inside address is just above the salutation, but, as in social correspondence, it may occasionally be placed after the close of the letter, at the left margin, two spaces below the level of the signature. This is not customary in ordinary business letters —only in those that are of an official nature—for instance, a letter to an officer of a club or to a government official, or perhaps in a letter which, while it deals with business, partakes of a personal flavor.

The Salutation

As mentioned in the section on personal letters, the term "salutation" means just that—a greeting at the beginning of your communication. The idea behind it is to avoid the abruptness that would otherwise mark the absence of such a preliminary step. If you begin without the salutation, you should seriously consider using an attention line indicating the nature of the letter (Re:) as a "buffer" between the inside address and the body of the letter.

When you know the name of the person to whom you are writing, use it. Write, "Dear Mr. Andrews," not "Dear Sir," except in cases of extreme formality.

When you don't know the name of the person to whom you are writing, then "Dear Madam or Sir" or

"Gentlemen or Mesdames" may be substituted for a name, although it is not a preferable beginning.

When you know the title of the person but not his or her name, you may write "Dear Marketing Director," but it does sound awkward and it would be preferable, if at all possible, to call the company and ask the name of the person with whom you are corresponding.

Although there are varying degrees of effusiveness which may be used in the salutation, from "Dear Mr. Jones" to "My very dear Mr. Jones," the preferable choice is simply "Dear . . ."

POSITION OF SALUTATION

The best position of the salutation is two spaces below the inside address, with the body of the letter beginning another two spaces below. This arrangement gives an appearance of compactness—an impression that the inside address, salutation, and body are all integral parts, which they are. It should begin exactly at the left margin, and a colon should follow it (unlike a personal letter, where the salutation is followed by a comma).

ATTENTION LINE

Now a word about what is sometimes called the *attention line*. It may be used to call special attention to the particular subject of the letter or to a company officer or employee whose special attention you desire in response to your letter. In the latter case, the idea is that you are writing not solely to the company nor to the individual, but to the company, with special emphasis on the fact that you wish the individual to give your letter a special reading.

Although this form is not widely used, it is acceptable. The form would be:

Barbara Riley, Ltd.
3 Elizabeth Drive
Westport, CT 06880

Attention: Mr. Colton Riley

Dear Sir or Madam:

It has come to my attention that, *etc.*

Note carefully that, if the attention line is used, the salutation is to the company, not to the individual named in the line—that is, "Dear Sir or Madam," not "Dear Mr. Riley." A mistake is frequently made in this respect.

We are giving considerable attention to the attention line because it is often implemented, and it should be used correctly. There is some justifiable doubt, however, as to its necessity. After all, a letter can be written to the company and, at the beginning, a special request can be made so that Mr. Brown gives it his personal attention. As for devoting a special attention line to the subject of the letter, that seems hardly necessary if the correspondence is directly to the point and well written. The nature and importance of the subject can and should be made clear very early in your letter.

In order to call attention to the special subject of the letter, it is customary to preface the subject with "Re:" (Latin for concerning), and to place it on a line between the inside address and the salutation.

The attention line can also serve as direction for your letter when you are not sure to whom you are writing. For example, if you are writing in response to an advertisement for a job and have no contact name, you could address your letter:

Box 568
Wall Street Journal
56 Wall Street
New York, NY 10011

Re: Executive Vice President Advertisement, June 30 edition

In response to your advertisement for executive vice president, *etc.*

This is particularly useful when you are reluctant to use the salutation "Dear Sir or Madam," etc., since it replaces the salutation.

The Body of the Letter

As already stated, single spacing is generally used in business letters. Although for very short letters double spacing is sometimes employed, it is not common. It is preferable to widen the margins, thereby narrowing the space across which the body of the letter is written. If, however, double spacing is used for a brief letter, paragraphs must be indented. Never use the block arrangement (flush with the margin) with double spacing. In the following discussion, we shall assume single spacing.

The body of the letter begins two spaces below the salutation. One has a choice between block or semiblock styles of set-up. Both are used a great deal, often block more than the other, and both give the same general appearance. In block arrangement, there is no indenting of paragraphs, each beginning at the left margin with a double space between paragraphs. In the semiblock set-up, the beginning of every paragraph is marked by an indention, varying from five to ten spaces, but usually five.

The principal placement of all the elements of a letter has to do with page balance, neatness, and pleasing appearance. Various adjustments of the factors mentioned may have to be made, according to the length of the letter. For example, a comparatively short letter with heading, date, inside address, and salutation all close to the top of the page, and an indention of only one inch for the block paragraphs, may leave too much of a margin at the bottom as to give a bare, unpleasing effect.

All those factors must be considered before the letter is typed in relation to how the letter will look after it has been completed. A high degree of proficiency will come with practice. The right-hand margin is established by the position of the date, which is typed to end flush with that margin, and by the length and desired placing of your letter on the page.

The Closing

A complimentary close to a letter is comparable to a few polite words of farewell at the conclusion of a business conference.

As in the case of all the other parts of the letter, the complimentary close should contribute to the general effect of pleasing balance. To that end, it is usually placed two spaces below the final line of the letter proper, and, unless the letter is set up to be aligned at the left margin, it begins in the center of the page, under the beginning of the date at the top of the letter, or the heading and date if the heading is not part of the stationery.

Depending on the length of the closing, you may have to go back to the top of the letter and adjust the beginning of the date. For example, *Very respectfully yours*, takes much more space than the more standard *Sincerely*, and therefore might be placed to the left of the center, while *Sincerely* may well be started slightly to the right of center.

For proper appearance, the complimentary close should not end far on the right-hand side of the page; it should never extend beyond the right-hand margin of the body. If a letter is very short, the complimentary close may be placed more than two spaces below the letter proper. If this is put into practice, however, be sure that the remainder of the letter is spaced and arranged in such a way that the close will not appear to be isolated.

In the complimentary close, do not capitalize any word except the first. "Yours very respectfully," is correct—not "Yours Very Respectfully," nor "Yours very Respectfully"; "Yours respectfully"—not "Yours Respectfully."

Never use the word respectively for respectfully. Perhaps the warning is entirely unnecessary, but the mistake is so frequently made, and so serious when it is made, that we mention it here.

Never use an abbreviation in the complimentary close. You cannot afford to do so, for any such absurdity as yrs. or Yrs. respectfully gives an impression not merely of carelessness but even more so of illiteracy.

Always end the complimentary close with a comma.

TYPES OF COMPLIMENTARY CLOSINGS

If you are very well acquainted with the person to whom you write on business matters, you may use a close that is quite informal. We shall concern ourselves here, however, only with the more frequent situation in which at least some degree of formality is in order. Although there is not a great variety among the various types of close, there are considerable choices according to the formality of your business letter.

A special point to be remembered is that, whatever complimentary close you use, it should be in keeping with the kind of salutation with which you open your letter. For example, if you use the formal and impersonal *Dear Sir or Madam* as an opening, you should close with a similarly formal *Truly yours* or *Very truly yours*, and not with a friendly, informal *Very cordially yours*.

It may be said that the close which omits *Yours* is less formal than the one which includes it; when *Yours* is included, it implies less formality when used at the beginning of the phrase than when used at the end. As basic words in the complimentary close, *cordially, sincerely, truly,* and *respectfully,* in the order here set down, indicate a gradation from the informal to the formal. When *very* is used with an informal close, it becomes still more formal; *very* used with a formal close makes it still more formal.

Among the following you will find the most commonly accepted forms of complimentary closings for business letters. Study them in relation to the principles explained above. Which of them would be best for very formal letters?

Cordially	Very truly yours
Cordially yours	Yours cordially
Respectfully	Yours respectfully
Respectfully yours	Yours sincerely
Sincerely	Yours truly
Sincerely yours	Yours very cordially
Truly yours	Yours very respectfully
Very cordially yours	Yours very sincerely
Very respectfully yours	Yours very truly
Very sincerely yours	

THE DOUBLE CLOSE

The participial ending, hanging in the air before the complimentary close, is not considered good usage: "Hoping that I may hear from you soon, I re-

main . . ." or "Trusting that this will meet with your
approval, I am . . ." If you have something like that to
say, make a sentence of it and then follow it with the
complimentary close proper:

I hope that I may hear from you soon.

                                    Very sincerely yours,

Your Signature

It is really astounding to note the weird and fantastic
symbols that often appear as signatures on business letters. They can no more be deciphered or "translated" by
the average reader than can hieroglyphics by the untu-
tored in Egyptology. All the worse, such signatures
sometimes appear with no typed duplicate under them,
and without the writer's name on the letterhead. In
brief, the reader may have no idea by whom the letter
has been sent.

In your own letters, even if your signature has been
typewritten under your writing, sign your name clearly
and evenly—not on a slant.

Three or four spaces should be left for the signature
between the complimentary close and the typed name.
Sometimes even more space is called for, if the signature
is large. Use single spacing for the last two lines (typed
name and title).

No part of the signature, neither the handwritten nor

the typed part, should run beyond the right-hand margin.

A person's title or position should never be placed on the same line as the handwritten signature.

Except for articles, conjunctions, and prepositions, all words stating the title, position, or rank of the signer should be capitalized. "The" is capitalized if it is an official part of the company name.

If circumstances prevent the writer from reading or signing the letter, the person who takes the responsibility for him or her should sign the writer's name and then type his own initials right under the signature. It is not necessary to use *per* before the initials.

Sincerely,

Richard B. Noonan
C.W.

Richard B. Noonan
Assistant Superintendent

The initials of the substitute signer may also be handwritten next to the signature rather than typed.

SIGNATURE AND RESPONSIBILITY

In business correspondence, the signature does more than merely indicate who wrote the letter. It indicates, too, who stands primarily responsible for what is written—the individual representing the company, or the company as such. If the company name is typed first, just above the personal signature, that means the company is primarily responsible for the content, and the individual only incidentally so.

> Very truly yours,
> Hawk Chemical Company
>
> *Andrew J. Smith*
>
> Andrew J. Smith
> Treasurer

If, on the other hand, the letter, on a company letterhead, is signed by an individual with his official standing typed below, perhaps with the firm name also typed underneath that, then the responsibility for the contents is his or hers.

> Very truly yours,
>
> *Linda Delli Colli*
>
> Linda Delli Colli, Treasurer
> Harrison Enterprises, Ltd.

Ending Information

IDENTIFICATION INITIALS

It is common practice, relative to the signature, to type the initials of the signer at the left-hand margin, two spaces below the level of the last part of the typed signature, and to follow these with a colon (sometimes a slash is preferred) and the initials of the typist: FLF:bjt.

Note that the signer's initials are capitalized and the typist's are lowercase. There is no punctuation between the letters of each set of initials.

ENCLOSURE

One space below, at the left margin, may be typed Enclosure if the letter includes one:

FLF:bjt
Enclosure

THE ''CARBON COPY''

Carbon paper to make copies of an original letter is practically extinct today, with word processors/computers able to print multiple copies at the push of a button or copy machines available to make as many copies as are required. The phrase "carbon copy" has remained, however, as an indication that a copy of the letter is being forwarded to another person or other persons. The lowercase letters "cc:" (followed by a colon) are typed two spaces beneath the identification initials, or below the word "Enclosure" if it is used. The name(s) of the persons to whom copies of the letter should be sent are typed at least two spaces to the right of the colon:

FLF:bjt
cc: Mrs. Altamuro
    Ms. Jensen
    Mr. Mignone

(First and last names, or first initials with the last name, may be used instead of titles, depending on the formality of the correspondence.)

A POSTSCRIPT

A postscript (P.S.) may serve a useful and legitimate purpose in briefly re-emphasizing something in the letter, or in calling attention to something that has a connection perhaps indirect but still important. Some maintain that a postscript should never be used, but this attitude seems unduly arbitrary.

If used, it should be brief. It may start at the left margin, two spaces above the identification initials, and the message should begin immediately after the "P.S." If the message runs for more than one line, the overrun should be indented where the message proper began:

P.S. You will note that our new Wisconsin office is strategically situated in relation to transportation.

The identification initials are then typed two spaces below the postscript message.

The Envelope

As with social correspondence, so with business letter writing are the completeness and clarity with which the envelope is addressed important factors. They are even more so in business than in social correspondence.

THE RETURN ADDRESS

First, be sure that you always have your return address on the envelope. This should be on the front, in the upper left-hand corner. You will remember that in social correspondence it may be on the back of the envelope (although this is not the preferred Post Office form), but for business letters the front is better. When business stationery is available, it is likely that envelopes have been printed to match. The envelopes generally include the company logo, the name of the company, the address, the city or town, state, and zip code. If they do not include your name, you may type your name and department below the last line of the printed envelope so that, if the letter is returned for some reason, the mail room personnel will be able to return it to you, unopened, for re-addressing. If you do not add your name, then someone will have to open the envelope (and likely read your letter) to determine to whom to return it.

NAME AND ADDRESS

The name and address of the person to whom you write should be placed halfway between the top and bottom of the envelope, or a little lower, and should be begun approximately in the center. Allow about half an inch between the address and the stamp.

If the street has a number—not a name—which consists of not more than two figures, you may spell it in full. For example, 324 First Street or 12 Sixteenth Street. This form looks better and makes easier reading than 324 1st Street or 12 16th Street. Of course, when the street number contains three figures, it is desirable to write it in figures: 42 125th Street.

The address is ordinarily written in three or four lines: name or name and title; company name; street address; city, state, and zip code.

In the past, when mail was processed by hand, the order of placement didn't make much difference. Today it does, since mail is processed mechanically and scanned by machine. The scanner, an optical character reader (OCR), is the computerized mail-processing system used nationwide, introduced to increase speed, efficiency, and accuracy in mail processing. The scanner reads an envelope from the bottom up, sorting each letter as it scans. Therefore, all notations that do not have anything to do with the address, such as "Personal," "Confidential," "Attention: T. Kellogg," a company logo, or "Invoice Enclosed," for example, may no longer be placed at the bottom of the envelope. Reading from the bottom, the last line should include the city or town, two letter abbreviation for the state, and the zip code. (See page 66 for state abbreviations.) The second to the last line should contain only the street number and address. The next line up is reserved for the name of the company, if applicable, with any building or floor destination (Rogers Publishing Group, 3rd floor). Above these lines, the notations mentioned previously may be typed or written to the left of the address block. The top line or two lines of the address is/are for the name and title of the recipient.

Other addressing guidelines from the Post Office are:

- Sans serif, simple typefaces should be used, since the scanners cannot read ornate typefaces.
- The scanners cannot read letters that touch, so proper spacing is important.
- If the address information is slanted or not within the standard addressing area, the scanners will not be able to read them.

Business envelopes should be typed in block, not indented format, with the return address in a block format, as well.

> Ms. Susan Foltin, President
> Life Resource Industries, Building G
> 655 Fourth Avenue South
> Minneapolis, MN 55415-9188

or

> *Confidential*
> Ms. Susan Foltin
> President
> Life Resource Industries, Building G
> 655 Fourth Avenue South
> Minneapolis, MN 55415-9188

WINDOW ENVELOPES

Window envelopes should not be used for formal correspondence of any sort, but are very efficient for such mailings as bills and form letters sent in bulk, since they eliminate the need for addressing an envelope. The only guideline is that you make sure the entire address can be read through the window. Letters or information inserted in window envelopes are folded in thirds with the first page of the letter, including the address, facing out instead of in.

ELECTRONIC CORRESPONDENCE

When liveried coachmen hopped into carriages and delivered the mail of the gentry by hand, correspondence was conducted by quill pen dipped in ink. Today, while some still hold on to their standard, nonelectric typewriters as their business writing vehicle of choice, and others have never relinquished their fountain pens and ink for social correspondence, still others have mastered at least three word-processing systems and have moved on to direct and instant communication via the facsimile (fax), electronic mail from one computer to another or a network of computers, and voice and image mail via audio and video tapes.

The earlier systems afforded some sense of privacy—the letters the coachmen carried were often closed by sealing wax—later letters were encased in envelopes held by gummed flaps, and still are today. Further privacy can be requested with the addition of the words "Confidential" or "Personal" added to the front of the envelope. The latter systems, however, are much more public and accordingly have some caveats associated with them. First, they should not be used to conduct personal business in a company setting nor to exchange confidential information, and second, they should have as professional an appearance as is expected for any other form of correspondence. Fast should not be equated with sloppy or unprofessional.

E-MAIL

E-Mail, or electronic mail, originates from one computer and is sent to the computer of a single designated person, or to a group of people, over the telephone system. Electronic mail can be sent across the country, or to an office on another floor of the same building. It doesn't use paper, unless the receiver prints a copy of the transmission on his or her printer. The communication is typed directly into the sender's computer; it is not reproduced from another document. It is encoded with the E-Mail numbers of the recipients and held in a computer file until they enter their systems and read the communication. A cost is generally incurred by the receiver for the time used to access E-Mail correspondence, so one should never send unessential communications through this system. It is not necessarily confidential or private unless encoded security systems are used.

More often than not, E-Mail correspondence is in the form of a memorandum, as described on page 28. The only differences between an electronic mail memo and one produced on a typewriter or word-processing system are that you obviously cannot sign them and that they are not received on any official memo stationery.

Some electronic mail is simply read on the computer screen of the recipient and then eliminated; some is printed out by the receiver who wants to keep a "hard" (paper) copy of your communication. He or she prints the copy onto whatever computer paper is in the printer.

Therefore, such technical details as spacing and margins are fairly irrelevant—the point of E-Mail is to transmit a message with alacrity, not to produce a communications work of art—and you generally start at the top of your screen and use whatever margins are built into the system. You should, however, still pay attention to spelling, sentence structure, punctuation, and paragraphing, and should begin the memo with the standard To/From/Regarding format.

State your message clearly and succinctly, whether it is to share information, to confirm an appointment, or to respond to a query. Double check for clarity and accuracy before you transmit.

FACSIMILE CORRESPONDENCE

The facsimile machine, universally called the fax, is an instant way to transmit a previously prepared letter or document. Like electronic mail, it depends on telephone lines to work. Also like electronic mail, the recipient needs compatible equipment to receive the transmission. Unless you are sending a facsimile copy to someone's home, which makes it a more private means of communication, or to someone's private office and you know your correspondence will be immediately accessible to them, the fax usually is centrally located within an office complex. Because of this, transmissions can be read by anyone who happens to be walking by the machine at the time your transmission is being sent. Marking the letter or document "Confidential" is fairly meaningless, since there is nothing confidential about the process. However it is received, our concern involves the way it is sent.

There are two forms of destination directions for fax transmissions. The first is referred to as a cover page. This page may be a sheet of company letterhead, or a form designed with lines or spaces to insert the name of the person to whom the transmission is directed (and his or her title or department, in a large company), your name, as sender, your telephone and/or fax number, the date, and the number of pages being sent. The cover page should be counted, as in "Cover +3." This information indicates to the recipient how many pages to expect so that, if you are sending a four-page document, plus the cover, and he or she receives only four pages in total, it will be obvious that a page is missing.

The second way to direct the destination of a fax is by means of a commercially produced self-adhesive form that is adhered to the first sheet being sent. This system saves using another piece of paper as a cover sheet, and is ecologically and economically more efficient. It may be, however, that the document being transmitted fills an entire page, in which case there is no room to affix the form and a separate cover sheet should be used, instead.

If a letter is being sent, it should be prepared exactly as any other business letter described in Chapter 2, including your signature. If the letter is being sent by fax because its contents require immediate attention but the "official" original will be required, you would mail the letter after transmitting it. When it is essential to know that it was sent by fax on a certain date and the original is a confirmation copy, type "Confirmation copy. Sent by fax 6/12/93" at the left margin under the identification initials described on page 47.

AUDIO TAPES

Generally a form of exchanging personal "electronic" letters to grandparents or other relatives who live a great distance away from you, audio tapes permit you to talk, at length, to the recipient—in essence, bringing a letter to life.

There are no particular rules for this form of letter, except that you naturally ascertain that the recipient has a tape player, and that you speak clearly.

Sometimes, executives will use audio tapes when talking through an idea, rather than holding extended telephone conversations with an associate at another location. If audio tapes are used for business purposes, you should state the date and the subject matter at the beginning of the tape; and if it is one of many or is to be preserved, affix a label to the tape which describes its contents.

VIDEO TAPES

Video tapes used for business purposes can provide clear descriptions or demonstrations of the information being communicated. For example, if you are scouting locations for a branch office in another town, you might tape the town and the proposed site so that others participating in the decision can review the location without actually having to travel to it with you. Or you can tape a meeting in progress where visual aides are being used so that associates not in attendance are able to review the content of the meeting and have access to the same presentation material.

Sending the videotape takes the place of what would have to be a very lengthy letter, but it should be treated as a "letter," without personal comments, jokes, background music, or unintelligible or extraneous information being added, which only detract from the intent of your communication.

As with audio tapes used for business purposes, the video tapes should be clearly and neatly labeled with the date and the subject matter, and, if possible, the approximate length, so that the recipient knows how much time to set aside to view it.

TECHNICALITIES

Two invaluable tools to every letter writer are a dictionary, when handwriting or typing correspondence, and a computer spell check, when using a word-processing system. Misspellings—along with errors in punctuation, usage, and other grammatical errors—add nothing to your effectiveness as a communicator and in fact distract the attention of the reader from the intended message.

Other technicalities—such as determining the correct title of the person to whom you are writing, using zip codes correctly, and knowing and using proper abbreviations—can only enhance your message and the image you wish to project.

ACCURACY IN SPELLING NAMES

In the matter of company names, follow the exact official form used by the company. If, for instance, the words "Company," "Corporation," or "Incorporated" are officially abbreviated, then follow that form in your inside address, as well as on the envelope—otherwise, spell it in full. Be very careful to spell the company name correctly. Few errors make a worse impression than a misspelled name.

This is perhaps even more important in the case of an individual. Everyone is touchy on this score. No one likes to have his name mistreated in any way—typographical errors, misspelling, or the use of any form other than the one the person himself or herself customarily employs. A man may sign his name in some way that strikes you as extremely informal for a business letter, so you decide to be properly formal. In replying to Jim Rooney's letter, you perhaps use the name James and create an impression that may harm your business relations. Let his signature be your guide, and you cannot go wrong.

SPELLINGS YOU SHOULD KNOW

Because good spelling plays an important part in effective letter writing, we include here a list of words whose spellings sometimes cause trouble. Although those who have little trouble with spelling may judge too harshly those who do have difficulty, the fact remains that your letters, whether social or business, are judged in no small degree by how well or how badly you spell.

Some people simply do not take the trouble to master certain words, since they believe the matter to be unimportant. That belief is far from the truth. Form, usage, expression—all of these are vital factors in good letter writing, but you may excel in all and still make a bad impression if your spelling is seriously deficient.

You will find the following list helpful if you make it a point to master any listed words that you ordinarily misspell. Concentrate on them, use them, spell them correctly, and you will improve your letter writing to a great extent.

abeyance	alias	bouquet
absorbent	allege	breathe
accede	allotment	bulletin
accelerate	annihilate	bureau
accessible	anonymous	calendar
accidentally	antedate	capital
accommodate	apologize	capitol
achievement	apparent	ceiling
acknowledgment	appreciate	census
acquiesce	arguing	changeable
adherence	attention	chauffeur
advantageous	authorize	chrysanthemum
advisable	baptize	clique
advise	benefitted	collectible
advisory	bequeath	comparatively
aggravate	bigoted	complementary

complimentary
concede
connoisseur
conscientious
consensus
contemptible
convalescence
convertible
corps
council
counselor
courtesy
criticize
cynic
debutante
deceased
delivery
dependent
desert
despondent
dessert
destructible
development
digestible
disagreement
disappointment
discernible
discreet
disheveled
dispel
donor
economize
eighth
eligible

embarrassing
en route
envelope
equipped
exaggerate
excusable
exhilarating
exquisite
extol
facetious
facsimile
faux pas
fiery
foreboding
forehead
foresight
forfeiture
franchise
frivolous
fulfill, fulfil
gauge
genteel
gnarled
gorgeous
grammatical
grievous
guarantee
gullible
hazard
hoping
hygiene
hypocrisy
illegible
imminent

impede
inadmissible
incidentally
indispensable
inflammable
intercede
interchangeable
irresistible
itinerary
jeopardize
judiciary
juvenile
khaki
knowledge
laboratory
laryngitis
legible
libel
license
loose
lose
luscious
maintenance
mantelpiece
mileage
mischievous
misspell
morale
motley
murmur
naive
nickel
niece
nonchalant

noticeable
nuisance
nutritious
obsession
occasionally
occurrence
omitted
ordinance
parallel
perceive
permissible
plaintiff
precede
pretense
prevalent
principle
procedure
profited
prophecy
prophesy
pseudo
pungent
pursuing
questionnaire
quietus
quizzes
quotient

recede
recommend
relieve
reservoir
respectfully
restaurant
rhythm
riddance
seize
separate
shipped
siege
sincerely
sinus
sleuth
stationary
stationery
stucco
suing
supersede
suspense
sycophant
syllable
symmetrical
synchronize
synonymous
tendency

tonsil
traceable
transference
treatise
trousseau
tryst
tyro
ukulele
umbrella
unanimous
unique
unnecessary
upbraid
vaccine
vacuum
vanilla
vendor
vengeance
veterinary
vetoes
vice versa
vicissitude
villainous
weird
whereas
withal

ABBREVIATIONS

Sometimes abbreviations are a matter of choice, but not always. The Post Office asks that we *always* abbreviate the following: Ave. (Avenue), Blvd. (Boulevard), St. (Street), Sq. (Square), and Bldg. (Building), because their scanners are programmed to read the abbreviations. While this helps speed mail to its destination, many prefer not to abbreviate, particularly in more formal correspondence. You may follow your wishes as to whether or not to abbreviate these words (but they should still be spelled out, in full, on formal invitations).

You may or may not abbreviate the following, as well: Hon. (Honorable), Rev. (Reverend), Rt. Rev. (Right Reverend), Prof. (Professor), Sec. (Secretary), Vice Pres. (Vice President), Pres. (President), Mgr. (Manager); and geographical location as part of an address, such as N. Chatsworth Ave. or W. 42nd Street.

The Post Office, again the authority on getting mail where it has to go as quickly as possible, requests that all states and territories be abbreviated on the envelope. The list of approved state abbreviations follows here. Note that these abbreviations contain no punctuation. The only restriction in abbreviating state names is on formal invitations, such as wedding invitations, where nothing is abbreviated. The choice is yours, however, on the inside address for your other personal and business correspondence.

There are certain well-known abbreviations that are standard. A few examples are: Mr., Mrs., Sr., Jr., and Esq. It looks decidedly odd to see Mr. spelled "Mister" as part of an address or salutation. Ms is not an abbreviation but rather a word created to give women the option not to have to indicate their marital status by their title.

Other standard abbreviations are C.O.D. (Collect on Delivery); F.O.B. (Freight on Board); A.V. (Authorized

Version); M.D. (Doctor of Medicine); Ph.D. (Doctor of Philosophy); C.P.A. (Certified Public Accountant); and organization initials, such as F.B.I. (Federal Bureau of Investigation) and A.M.A. (American Medical Association). These are more ordinarily seen as abbreviations than they are seen spelled out.

State/Territory Abbreviations

Alabama	AL	Mississippi	MS
Alaska	AK	Missouri	MO
Arizona	AZ	Montana	MT
Arkansas	AR	Nebraska	NE
California	CA	Nevada	NV
Colorado	CO	New Hampshire	NH
Connecticut	CT	New Jersey	NJ
Delaware	DE	New Mexico	NM
District of Columbia	DC	New York	NY
Florida	FL	North Carolina	NC
Georgia	GA	North Dakota	ND
Guam	GU	Ohio	OH
Hawaii	HI	Oklahoma	OK
Idaho	ID	Oregon	OR
Illinois	IL	Pennsylvania	PA
Indiana	IN	Puerto Rico	PR
Iowa	IA	Rhode Island	RI
Kansas	KS	South Carolina	SC
Kentucky	KY	South Dakota	SD
Louisiana	LA	Tennessee	TN
Maine	ME	Texas	TX
Maryland	MD	Utah	UT
Massachusetts	MA	Vermont	VT
Michigan	MI	Virginia	VA
Minnesota	MN	Washington	WA

West Virginia	WV	Wyoming	WY
Wisconsin	WI		

PUNCTUATION

Since punctuation is essential to good letter writing, either social or business, and is called for even on the envelope, we shall briefly review the minimum requirements. You may well refer to this section often and to advantage, and, when you come to the examples of good letters (in Parts Two and Three of this book), you may compare them with the principles explained here. In that way you will not only become familiar with good punctuation but will also fix in your mind the reasons for each form—the best possible way to remember the forms.

Much has been written about hard-and-fast rules of punctuation. In this book, we wish to emphasize the simple idea that one should concentrate on the *meaning* and forget about rules. Good punctuation in letters carries with it certain additional meanings and inflections that are not conveyed in the word symbols themselves. It often serves the same purpose as voice inflection in speech. For example, note the difference of meaning in the following, according to the punctuation: "We won." "We won?" "We won!"

From the standpoint of meaning, therefore—one definite meaning for each punctuation mark—good punctuation is easy to master. Thoroughly understand the meaning of each mark, fix it firmly in mind, and then use punctuation to write exactly what you mean. In the following pages, you will find an explanation of what each mark means and an illustration of its correct usage.

Beginning and End Punctuation

This is used to show the reader where one sentence ends and another begins. Without it, sentences would run together in a hopeless jumble. Four familiar marks are used to separate sentences.

THE PERIOD

This means "A complete sentence ends here." Do not confuse it with the abbreviation point, which is used for an incomplete word symbol (Oct. for October, Y.M.C.A.); or with the decimal point, which is used with certain figures (5.25); or with the comma-like symbol used to separate the parts of large numbers (450,000).

THE EXCLAMATION POINT

This mark means that the idea immediately preceding is to be given great emphasis. In speaking, you might provide similar emphasis by adding a remark such as, "You have to be kidding!" The exclamation point has the same effect in writing. Do not make too free use of this mark. The exclamation point should be reserved for really important occasions.

THE QUESTION MARK

As the name implies, the question mark indicates the end of a sentence that asks a question: "Where are you going?" Note that a whole question may sometimes be implied, and very effectively, in one word: "Honestly?" (Do you honestly mean that?)

THE BEGINNING CAPITAL LETTER

This symbol means "A new sentence starts here." It marks the start of a new sentence just as the period marks the end. (Summer is my favorite time of year. Seeing everything in bloom makes me happy.)

SENTENCE FRAGMENTS

There are certain sentence fragments, or incomplete statements, that make sense by themselves and which are very commonly used (a word, phrase, dependent clause). In any such case, treat the fragment like a complete sentence, and use appropriate beginning and end punctuation. Thus: "Not a chance." "Help!" "Why that?" Do not overdo sentence fragments. In each case, make sure your meaning is clear.

The Five Principal Interior Marks

Besides the beginning and end punctuation, explained above, there are five principal interior punctuation marks.

Inside the sentence, especially if it is long, sometimes

the words alone cannot make the meaning perfectly clear. Thus, for clarification, we use various punctuation marks. Three of the five basic marks consist of the comma symbol, either alone or in combination. Each, however, is a separate mark with a distinct meaning of its own.

THE SINGLE COMMA

This means "Here a small element has been omitted." It is used comparatively seldom, and the reader can always supply the omitted element easily for himself: "To advance was difficult; to retreat, impossible." Substituting the small element (was) for the comma, the sentence would read, "To advance was difficult; to retreat was impossible." The sentence "He was bright, articulate, witty." has a comma representing an "and" that has been omitted. In such a series sometimes an "and" is used before the last word of the series, for smoother reading; but even then it is better to insert the extra single comma: "He was bright, articulate, and witty." Some editors omit the final comma. Note especially, however, that when any element in the series is a compound, the final comma is necessary. Thus: "She had red, pink and green, yellow, and gold balloons." If the final comma here were omitted, you would have "yellow and gold balloons," which might mean a combination of color. In brief, it seems best always to use the final comma.

THE PAIR OF COMMAS

Perhaps the most important punctuational symbol, this is the most frequently used of all marks of interior punctuation. It means "The element set off by this pair of commas is not essential to the grammatical sentence structure, and, as placed, changes the normal order."

An English sentence has the following normal order: subject, with essential modifiers; verb, with essential modifiers; and object or verb complement, with essential modifiers. Now, you must use commas to "flag," or warn, the reader when you depart from the normal order by inserting a nonessential element. This is particularly important to remember because, owing to the structure of the English language, there are many and various instances of nonessential elements that break into and interrupt the normal syntax, or construction, and which therefore require the pair of commas. The following are typical examples of the principal cases:

1. Nonrestrictive clauses require the pair of commas. Such clauses interrupt the normal order.

   Examples: (a) The Assistant Superintendent, who was also Treasurer, was always present at the meeting of the Board. (The dependent clause, separated by commas, does modify the subject but is not an essential modifier. The sentence would be perfectly clear if it were omitted. It breaks the normal order by separating subject from verb. Hence the pair of commas.) (b) She considered Barry, who had always encouraged her, the best boss she had.

Note, however, that restrictive clauses, essential to the meaning, are not set off by commas.

Examples: (a) The friend who is not loyal is no friend at all. (The dependent clause in this case, too, stands between subject and verb but, since it is an essential modifier of the subject, there is no violation of the normal order. Hence, the pair of commas is not used.) (b) She shook hands with the man who was to be her partner.

2. Words in apposition are always nonessential, interruptive elements and therefore call for the pair of commas.

Examples: (a) Mrs. John Ferguson, the hostess, gave a speech of welcome. (b) The Reverend Marvin Henk, the school chaplain, officiated at the dedication.

3. Transitional phrases and words are merely connecting links between one idea and another. With no grammatical function, and no normal sentence position, they always separate two elements that belong together.

Examples: (a) This candidate, in brief, is the best. (b) The curriculum, we believe strongly, should be adopted immediately.

4. Words, names, or titles used in direct address are nonessential and always interrupt the normal order.

Examples: (a) This, Mrs. Roode, is the way the new system works. (b) Wait, Annette, while I get my coat. (c) Here, Dr. Bott, is the new student.

5. Conventionally regarded as grammatically nonessential elements interrupting the normal order are: the figure for a year immediately following a date within that year; and the name of a geographical area immediately following the name of a part of that area.

Examples: (a) She was born on July 2, 1981, at eight in the morning. (b) His address is 219 Hornbine Road, Rehoboth, Massachusetts.

6. A direct quotation within a sentence is also regarded as a nonessential, interruptive element, although this usage seems purely arbitrary and conventional. A pair of commas is used.

Examples: (a) Nathan Hale uttered his immortal words, "I only regret that I have but one life to lose for my country," as the hangman's noose settled about his neck. (b) He was shouting, "I am innocent," as they led him from the courtroom.

It should be carefully noted that when the nonessential interruptive element comes at either the beginning or the end of the sentence, only one part of a pair of commas is used. The other comma is absorbed, or replaced, by the beginning or the end punctuation.

Examples: (a) Without a doubt, this is an excellent opportunity. (b) She is no wonder woman, for all that.

Such nonessential elements (word, phrase, clause) change the normal order because, as emphasized earlier, normally the first thing in the sentence is the subject with its essential modifiers, and the last thing is the object or verb complement with its essential modifiers. Note the following sentences.

Examples: (a) When he had turned off the air conditioner, he left his office for the night. (b) He left his office for the night when he had turned off the air conditioner. (No commas are used in the second example, because the modifying clause is in its normal position, exactly where it belongs.)

THE COMMA PLUS COORDINATING CONJUNCTION

This is a mark normally used in only one situation, namely, in the middle of a compound sentence. It means "One independent clause has now been completely stated, and another is about to begin."

Examples: (a) She has done her best, but she has failed. (b) We are looking forward to the championship, for we have worked hard all year.

THE SEMICOLON

This is a mark that has practically the same meaning as the comma plus coordinating conjunction. Either may be used to indicate the midpoint of a compound sentence.

Examples: (a) She has done her best; she has failed. (b) We are looking forward to the championship; we have worked hard all year.

In the use of the semicolon, however, there are two important variations:

1. If a sentence is complicated, a semicolon plus conjunction may sometimes be used instead of a comma plus conjunction for the purpose of clarification, especially if the sentence includes a considerable number of commas and therefore might be confusing if a semicolon were not used.

   Example: The twilight was alive with a weird collection of bird, animal, and insect life, including great bats, swift and terrible, that swooped down on us without warning; and, as darkness fell, we were treated, if that is the word, to a symphony from an insect orchestra which, to say the least, was slightly out of tune.

2. If the elements in a series are long and complicated, one may sometimes use a semicolon instead of a comma (which indicates the omission of a conjunction between elements in a series).

   Example: He had a record of three years as a social studies teacher, filled with challenges presented by classes of students with mixed abilities; four years as a high school principal, where, quite unexpectedly, he found himself receiving national attention for his methods; and, as a climax, a brilliant career as the state education commissioner, where, for the duration, he continued to extol the virtues of dedication for the achievement of educational excellence.

THE COLON

This is equivalent to "in other words," "namely," "that is." It means "What follows will explain more fully what has just been said."

Examples: (a) This was the quandary: she could begin a totally new career, or stay where she was and hope for additional promotions. (b) The store contained just four departments: housewares, plumbing accessories, garden equipment, and lawn furniture. (c) His achievement was remarkable: he had risen to great heights, in spite of handicaps that others had considered insurmountable.

It is customary to use a colon after the salutation at the beginning of a formal speech or letter, and after the word "Resolved," introducing a resolution, as in the case of a subject for a debate. All this is a matter of formal convention, rather than that of punctuation. Note also its use after the word "Examples," as employed in this discussion:

Examples: (a) Dear Mrs. Marino: (b) Madame Chair, Ladies and Gentlemen: (c) Resolved: That the Board adopt a budget that does not increase over this year's budget.

Other Marks of Punctuation

These marks possess considerable importance, even though they are less frequently used.

THE SINGLE DASH

This mark means exactly the reverse of the colon, namely: "This is a summary or condensation of the details just given." In other words, the detailed statement precedes the dash.

Examples: (a) She could consolidate the two departments and make them one, or she could hire a new manager for the second department—these were her best options. (b) A desk, a chair, a file cabinet and a telephone—just these four articles the office contained. (c) He had risen to great heights in spite of handicaps that others had considered insurmountable—his achievement was remarkable.

PARENTHESES

When used to enclose any element in a sentence, parentheses mean: "The normal order of the sentence is here changed by the insertion of a nonessential element so phrased that it bears little or no grammatical relationship to the rest of the sentence." Parentheses are much stronger marks than the pair of commas. They mark a more abrupt break in the sentence with respect to the relationship between the elements.

Examples: (a) The entire Board of Directors (15 members, in all) traveled to the shareholder's meeting in the company van. (b) The whole school (1,827 pupils, that year) was struck by the epidemic.

PAIR OF DASHES

This punctuation mark indicates an emphatic break. It says, as it were, "Here occurs a violent interruption, either emotional or syntactical, that disrupts the normal order."

Example: The swift onset of the flood—the waters had risen six feet in as many hours—drove the inhabitants rushing from the town.

It should be carefully noted that sometimes only one-half of the pair of dashes is used. Such is the case when a sentence is violently broken off, never to be completed.

Example: "Help! Help!" shouted the man on the ledge. "I can't—" The roar of the collapsing building drowned the rest.

QUOTATION MARKS

As the term implies, these credit some person or other source with the material enclosed by the marks. They mean "The enclosed element consists of the exact words of some person or other source that the author is quoting." Single quotation marks are used for a quotation within quotation, within the second one, double marks are again used. Other principal uses of quotation marks are: to enclose titles of magazine articles, slang used in formal writing, and ordinary words or expressions used in a special sense.

Examples: (a) "I shall quote," said the prosecutor, "the very words he used: 'I'll see you dead, first.'" (b) "Our neighbor," said my grandfather, "used to say, 'My son always was quoting the Shakespearean line, "To thine own self be true."'" (Note that the sentence ends with three sets of quotation marks.) (c) Her article, "The Life and Times of Barry Bennett Farnham," appeared in a leading magazine. (d) They call their house "the peaceable kingdom" because of all the pets who live together amicably.

BRACKETS

These are used to enclose, within a quotation, an explanatory remark made, not by the speaker himself or herself, but by the person who is quoting the speaker.

Example: The speaker went on, "My nomination of Kate Newberry [she is the incumbent chairperson] is based on the privilege of over ten years of serving on committees she has directed."

If you should ever feel that parentheses within parentheses are called for, use brackets instead of the inner pair of parentheses, to prevent confusion.

ELLIPSES

Ellipses, more recognizable when referred to as three dots, indicate the omission of material from a quotation, generally because the part omitted is not considered essential to the particular context. They mean "Here a certain part is omitted purposely, but without any suggestion of an abrupt or violent break." Contrast this with the dash, explained earlier.

Examples: (a) The report commends the company for "extraordinary attention to detail, exemplary personnel management . . . superb financial controls" and concludes with a commendation for the president. (b) "I seem to be very tired, and I . . ." His voice faded away and he was asleep.

SOME NONPUNCTUATIONAL DEVICES

Nonpunctuational devices include the hyphen and the apostrophe, as well as the abbreviation point and the decimal point discussed earlier under the heading "The Period."

THE HYPHEN

Two or more words are joined into a compound word by means of this spelling symbol; it is also used at the end of a line when a word is broken into syllables.

Examples: (a) a two-by-four plank. (b) he had a wonderful surprise awaiting him. (c) forty-five.

THE APOSTROPHE

This is another spelling symbol. It is used in contractions, possessives, and some plurals.

Examples: (a) don't; (b) the President's car; (c) the patrons' lounge; (d) three A's.

COMMON FAULTS IN USAGE

Just as in everyday conversation one is often surprised, and sometimes jarred, by errors in the use of the English language, so in both social and business letters many instances of bad usage occur. The following list includes some of the most objectionable common errors. In each example given below, proper usage is represented by the word (or words) in italics, and the use of the alternative word (or words) would be incorrect.

Adopt (adapt). Adopt means to make one's own, to accept. Adapt means to make to conform with, to adjust to.

Example: I shall *adapt* my paragraph style to indented form.

Affect (effect). Affect is a verb which means to exert influence upon. Effect, the verb, means to make something a reality, to bring about.

Example: The mediators *effected* a settlement.

All ready (already). All ready means entirely prepared. Already means before now, by this time.

Example: She had *already* left by the time he arrived.

All right (alright). The one-word spelling of all right is not correct.

Example: If the entire group agrees, it is *all right* with me, too.

At about (about). At refers to an exact place or time. About means approximate. At and about should never be used together.

Examples: He arrived *about* four o'clock. He left *at* six o'clock.

But what, but that (that). Generally this error is made in connection with the word "doubt." The inclusion of "but" is incorrect.

Example: There is little doubt *that* he will succeed.

Can't hardly (can hardly). Can't hardly involves a double negative and is therefore incorrect.

Example: I can *hardly* do it without help.

Continue on (continue). The on is unnecessary, for continue means to go on.

Example: I think the storm will *continue* into the night.

Could care less (Couldn't care less). Could care less means that you indeed, care, while couldn't care less, which is correct, means literally that you could not care less than you do; that you don't care at all.

Example: He thinks I am upset that he is leaving, but I *couldn't care less*.

Different than (different from). Although <u>different</u> <u>than</u> is perhaps the more often used of these two expressions, it is, none the less, bad usage.

Example: Your viewpoint is certainly *different from* his.

Don't (doesn't). Don't is a contraction of "do not" (plural); <u>doesn't</u> is a contraction of "does not" (singular).

Example: It *doesn't* seem right.

Due to (because of). <u>Due to</u> means owing to, or attributable to, something. It is used as an adjective, never as an adverb. <u>Because of</u> is used as an adverb.

Examples: His absence was *due to* an illness. He was absent *because of* illness.

Equally as (equally). The <u>as</u> is superfluous.

Example: The two men are *equally* skillful.

Every one . . . are (every one . . . is). The words <u>every one</u> are a singular construction and take a singular verb. Do not let intervening plurals deceive you.

Example: Every one of the two hundred animals *is* well fed.

First began (began). The word <u>first</u> is redundant and should not be used.

Example: She *began* her political career when barely out of college.

Free gratis (free or gratis). Since gratis is the Latin word for free, the two words should not be used together. Either free or gratis, alone, is correct.

Example: The sample from the store was free.

Generally always (generally or always). These two words are often used together when always alone is meant. Together, they make no sense.

Example: He generally arrives on time.

Greatly minimize (minimize). Minimize means to reduce to the very least. Since you cannot do more than that, greatly is incorrect.

Example: You minimize your contributions to this project.

I (me). Most often misused with the conjunction "and," as in "She gave the report to Jim and I." To determine whether this is correct, simply remove the "Jim and." Would you say, "She gave the report to I"? We think not.

Example: She gave the report to Jim and me.

Infer (imply). Infer means to draw a conclusion from someone else's action or statement. Imply, quite to the contrary, means to give someone else a basis on which to found a conclusion.

Example: I infer from his comments that he is not happy with the job Susan is doing. He implied that she was not completing assignments on time.

Know as (know that or know whether). The as makes no sense and is entirely out of place here.

Example: I don't know *that* (or know *whether*) this is a good idea.

Less (fewer). Less must not be used when the reference is to number. It is correct only when reference is made to amount or quantity.

Example: This year we had *fewer* mosquitoes than last.

Liable (likely, apt). A very common error is made in the use of these words. Liable in this context means culpable, responsible, answerable, or accountable. Likely simply refers to the strong possibility of an occurrence.

Example: It is *likely* to be a sunny day tomorrow.

Like (as). Like, when a verb, means to enjoy, esteem, appreciate, and admire. When an adjective, it means comparable, or similar. It never means "as," but it is astonishing how often it is misused in this context.

Example: *As* I said, I will not be able to attend.

Me (my). Before a verbal noun, or gerund, the objective case is incorrect. The possessive is required.

Example: Will the manager approve of *my* making this change in the order? (Other correct forms, instead of *my*, would be *your*, *his*, *our*, and *their*, never *him*, *her*, or *them*.)

Morning at A.M. (morning, A.M.) To use both in referring to the time is to repeat oneself, since A.M. means "in the morning."

Examples: The office opens at 9 A.M. The office opens at nine in the *morning*. (Not at 9 a.m. in the morning.)

Nothing else but (nothing but). The "else" is unnecessary.

Example: *Nothing but* perfection is his ideal.

People (persons). People is correctly used only in a collective reference to a comparatively large group.

Example: Two or three *persons* saw the accident.

Providing (provided). Providing is not allowable for expressing a conditional arrangement or situation.

Example: I will go, *provided* I can bring a friend.

Reason is [or was] because (reason is [or was], that). Because should not be used, since reason in itself implies because. It calls for a "that" clause explaining what the reason is or was.

Example: He was defeated in the election. The *reason is that* he presented his case poorly.

Shall (will) and will (shall). Misuses of these words, which are responsible for some of the most common errors in usage, should be strictly avoided. Shall is used in the first person, singular, and plural to express futurity or expectation; will in the second and third persons. Just the reverse is true when command or determination is to be expressed. In questions, it is correct to use the form that is logically to be expected in the answer.

Examples: I *shall* be leaving early. I think you *will* have trouble getting home on time. You *shall* do as I say. We *shall* depend on you. We *will* defend our principles to the last. *Shall* you be staying here long? (The answer expected is, "I shall" or "shall not.")

Stop (stay). Stop refers to cessation of previous motion or procedure, and should be only so used.

Example: He expects me to *stay* here a week.

These (this) kind. There is really little excuse for making this very common mistake—using a plural modifier with a singular noun.

Example: *This kind* is made in Canada.

Try and (try to). Try and clearly implies that one accomplishes what he tries. Try to means something quite different. One may try to do something, but not succeed.

Example: I'll *try to* be there on Saturday.

Uninterested (disinterested). Uninterested means having or showing no interest in. Disinterested means impartial, unprejudiced.

Example: A good judge is *disinterested* in the cases that he tries.

Wait (await). These words are not synonymous. Wait means simply to stay, to remain. Await means to wait for, and generally there is an implication of something important about to happen.

Example: He decided to *await* further developments.

Want to (ought to, should). Want to is a peculiar usage in this sense which, if analyzed literally, makes very little sense. It is a colloquialism that should be strictly avoided.

Example: You *should* be very careful.

HACKNEYED PHRASES

We all know individuals who seem to have no originality of expression. They use one stale phrase after another. Hardly any of us, however, can "cast the first stone," for we, ourselves, may be guilty in a greater or lesser degree. For that reason we are presenting here some of the most overworked expressions. With these as a warning, no doubt you will recognize and avoid many others also.

You will note that not all the expressions given in our list are always to be avoided. But, by and large, the list represents usage worn out through old age and hard service. We have set them down at random, believing that it will be of interest to you to take them in no special order and, as you come to each, check your own tendency to use it.

I note from your letter
I note that
Please note
Let me point out
Please rest assured
Permit me to say
Has come to hand
May I suggest
I take pleasure
I note with pleasure
I regret to state
How nice to hear from you
With your kind permission
Please do not hesitate
Please be informed
I wish to inform
This will inform you
Attached please find
Enclosed herewith
Enclosed please find
Herewith please find
Thank you kindly
Thanking you for your courtesy
Trusting this will find you well
Acknowledge with thanks
In reply, I would say
I have before me
In this connection
At the present writing
I carefully noted

At the earliest possible moment
At an early date
At your earliest convenience
That's the kicker
A tough nut to crack
Hoping this finds you well
Kindly advise me
Along this line
For your information
At hand
Awaiting your reply
Thanking you in advance
Up to this writing
in re
as per
In the not too distant future
Pleasure of a reply
In due time
Kindly inform
Take this opportunity
Keep in touch
Await the pleasure of a reply
Your letter of recent date
Referring to your favor
Wherein you state
Said person stated
Have attended to same
Come to closure
Hoping to hear from you
Drop me a line
What's new
Take care

Part Two

TYPES OF SOCIAL LETTERS

Invitations and Announcements

Through the years, the invitations used for all but the most formal of occasions—weddings, balls, graduations, bar and bat mitzvah's, for example—have taken the form of preprinted, fill-in invitations which are widely available. Whatever the form, it is essential, for the desired impression, that an invitation or announcement be correct and the content gracious and pleasing. Even with informal invitations, the degree of informality will depend on the nature of the occasion and the closeness of relationship between the writer and the recipient.

The important elements are those of clarity—date, time, purpose, and degree of formality—which let the recipient know what is expected of him or her, and what to expect.

Unless otherwise indicated, a response is always expected, and should be in like form. Only when the invitation reads "regrets only," which means the recipient need respond only if he or she cannot attend, is no response necessary when the reply is favorable.

A formal, third-person invitation requires a formal, third-person reply unless a response card is enclosed with the invitation. An informal note of invitation requires a written or telephone response so that the sender knows to expect those who have been invited. In both cases, the response should be immediate. In all cases, as with replies to all invitations, the response should repeat the date and time of the event as a confirmation that it was stated and understood correctly.

WEDDING INVITATIONS AND REPLIES—FORMAL

Wedding Invitations—Formal

Most formal wedding invitations are engraved or printed. In such cases, a good stationer should be consulted.

Mr. and Mrs. Eric Stockmar
request the honour of your presence
at the marriage of their daughter
Linda
to
Mr. Paul Degenhardt
Saturday, the seventh of October
at half after five o'clock
Larchmont Avenue Church
Larchmont, New York

WITH RECEPTION CARD ENCLOSED

Reception
immediately following the ceremony
Larchmont Yacht Club
Larchmont
The favour of a reply is requested
34 Linwood Avenue
New Rochelle, New York 10601

INVITATION TO RECEPTION ONLY

When the wedding ceremony is private and a large reception is held, the invitation to the ceremony is given orally or extended by personal note, and an invitation to the reception is mailed.

Mr. and Mrs. John Moller
request the pleasure of your company
at the wedding reception of their daughter
Samantha Jane
and
Mr. Shawn William Amdur
Saturday, the fifteenth of May
at three o'clock
Orienta Beach Club
Rehoboth Beach, Maryland
R.S.V.P.

INVITATION TO CEREMONY AND RECEPTION IN ONE

When all guests are to be invited to both the ceremony and the reception, the invitation may be com-
bined as one.

Mrs. Charlene Walter
requests the honour of your presence
at the marriage of her daughter
Kristin Marie
to
Mr. Peter Anders Wadsworth
Church of the Resurrection
Kittery
and afterward at the reception
Mount Heather Country Club
The favour of a reply is requested
12 Smithston Lane
Kittery, Maine 03904

INVITATION TO A HOME WEDDING

Mr. and Mrs. Arthur Newberry
request the honour of your presence
at the marriage of their daughter
Virginia Ann
to
Mr. Gary Allan Wollen
on Monday, the first of June
at half after five o'clock
5 Prade Lane
Massapequa Park, New York
R.S.V.P.

Replies to Wedding Invitation—Formal

Dr. and Mrs. Reid William Coleman
accept with pleasure
Mr. and Mrs. Arthur Newberry's
kind invitation to be present at the
marriage of their daughter
Virginia Ann
to
Mr. Gary Allan Wollen
Monday, the first of June
at half after five o'clock

Mr. and Mrs. Steven Hagstrom
regret exceedingly that they
are unable to accept
Mr. and Mrs. Arthur Newberry's
kind invitation to be present at the
marriage of their daughter
Virginia Ann
to
Mr. Gary Allen Wollen
Monday, the first of June
at half after five o'clock

Cancellation of Invitation—Formal

Mr. and Mrs. Thomas Tobin
announce that the marriage of
their daughter
Susannah
to
Mr. Rolf Helman
will not take place

WEDDING INVITATIONS AND REPLIES— INFORMAL

Wedding Invitations—Informal

When a wedding is informal, the invitations should match that informality and be extended by note or letter. They may be written by the bride's parents or by the bride or groom themselves.

TO A RELATIVE

Dear Aunt Ruth,
    On Wednesday, June the twelfth, at six o'clock, Brad and I will be married in the chapel at St. Peter's on 54th Street.
    Please say you will be there with us, and after the wedding for dinner at the Ambassador Club.

Brad sends his love, and we both are in high hopes that you will be with us on the twelfth!

With love,
Erin

TO A FRIEND

Dear Rick,

You are among the first people to whom we are telling our news—Todd and I are getting married, and the date and place have been set. The wedding will be at the Fifth Avenue Church at three in the afternoon, April 6th, and there will be a reception at my parents' house afterward. Both the ceremony and the party will be a simple, small gathering of our most special friends and relatives. Because you are one of our most special friends, we would be so happy if you were with us. Please say yes!

In hopes that you will, there are directions to the church enclosed.

Affectionately,
Kathleen

TO A FRIEND

Dear Trudy,

Hank and I have decided on Thursday, June the sixth, as the date for our wedding. We both want an extremely simple ceremony and are hoping our two closest friends (you, and Hank's friend, Rob) will act as our witnesses. The ceremony will be at 3:30 at my house, and later some other friends and relatives will join us for a small reception.

I couldn't get married without you there, Trudy!

Love,
Amanda

FROM THE BRIDE'S MOTHER

Dear Mr. and Mrs. Southwick,

We are hoping you will honor us with your presence at Becky's and Evan's wedding October the fifteenth at three o'clock. The ceremony and reception will be at our home in Kent, with Becky's and Evan's closest and favorite friends in attendance. They number you among those friends, and my husband and I are in hopes that you will be able to be with us. We look forward to meeting you and to sharing this special afternoon with you.

                                        Sincerely,
                                        Roslyn Sandler

Replies to a Wedding Invitation—Informal

RELATIVE'S ACCEPTANCE

Dearest Erin,

You have no idea how delighted I am with your news! I grew so fond of Brad when you two visited last summer, and have been hoping a wedding was in your future.

Of course I will be there, and at the reception, too. And I'll look forward to hearing all the family news.

Please give my love to your mother and father, and to Brad. I'll see you soon.

                                        Lovingly,
                                        Aunt Ruth

FRIEND'S REGRET

Dear Kathleen,

It is with great regret that I write to tell you that I won't be able to be with you and Todd on the fifth of April. Up until I received your letter I had been considering myself very lucky that the bank was sending me to Australia on business—now I'd give anything to stay home.

Please know I'll be with you in thought—and will call when I return to see when you and Todd can join me for a celebration dinner.

> Fondly,
> Rick

FRIEND'S ACCEPTANCE

Dear Amanda,

Of course I will be with you and Hank on June the sixth, and I am so honored that you have asked me to be your witness—remember how we always said we'd be in each other's weddings, when we were little? It's our dream come true, and I look forward to the reception and a chance to spend a little time together.

I'll be counting the days.

> Love,
> Trudy

BRIDAL SHOWERS—INVITATIONS AND REPLIES

Shower—Letter of Invitation

Dear Allison,

When last we spoke, we talked about Carrie's forthcoming marriage, and I mentioned I was hoping to give a shower for her. Indeed, I am, and would be delighted if you could attend.

The shower will be at my house on Sunday, August the seventh, at two o'clock. It's a bed and bath shower, and Carrie's color theme is blue and white.

We're trying to keep it a surprise, so don't say anything when you next see Carrie! Hope you'll be able to attend.

Cordially,
Sally

Shower—Letter of Acceptance

Dear Sally,

It will be a pleasure to be one of Carrie's friends at the shower you are giving for her. Thank you for including me —I am looking forward to being at your home on Sunday, the seventh, at two o'clock.

Cordially,
Allison

Shower—Letter of Regret

Dear Sally,

It is with real regret that I must decline your wonderful invitation to Carrie's shower. We are expecting houseguests the weekend of the seventh, and I will need to stay with them. I will send a gift for Carrie to your house, and would appreciate it if you could give it to her, with my love.

Thank you for inviting me. I'll be thinking of all of you on the seventh.

Affectionately,
Maryann

INVITATIONS TO DINNER AND REPLIES— FORMAL

Invitation to Dinner—Formal

Mr. and Mrs. Richard McMillan
request the pleasure of
Miss Molly Dillon's company
at dinner
on Friday evening, September the ninth
at seven o'clock
1823 Kenwood Parkway
Minneapolis

R.S.V.P.

Acceptance—Formal

Miss Molly Dillon
accepts with pleasure
the kind invitation of
Mr. and Mrs. Richard McMillan
for dinner
on Friday, the ninth of September
at seven o'clock

Regret—Formal

Mr. and Mrs. Mark Dillon
regret that they are unable to accept
the kind invitation
of
Mr. and Mrs. Richard McMillan
for Friday, the ninth of September

Invitation to Dinner, Formal, To Meet a Special Guest

Mr. William Ackerman
requests the pleasure of
Mr. and Mrs. Michael O'Connel's company
at dinner
on Wednesday, March the third
at seven o'clock
to meet Mrs. Arian Coan
140 Osborn Road
Goldens Bridge

R.S.V.P.

Invitation to Dinner, on a Special Occasion—Formal

Mr. and Mrs. Gerald Havlin
request the pleasure of your company
at dinner
on the Tenth Anniversary of their marriage
Saturday, the twelfth of May
at eight o'clock
Bellhaven Yacht Club
Greenwich
The favour of a reply
is requested

Invitation to Dinner and Theater—Formal

Mr. Frank O'Gorman
requests the pleasure of
Mr. and Mrs. Leonard D'Appolito's company
for dinner and theater
on Thursday, July the sixth
at half after six o'clock
30 East 37th Street
New York
Kindly respond

Cancellation of Dinner Invitation—Formal

Mr. and Mrs. Gerald Havlin
announce with regret that
owing to sudden illness
they are obliged to recall
their invitation for dinner
on
Saturday, May the twelfth

FORMAL ANNOUNCEMENTS

Wedding announcements are sent to those who have not
received invitations to a wedding, anywhere from the
day after the wedding up to but no later than one year
from the day of the wedding.

Wedding Announcement from the Bride's Parents—Formal

Mr. and Mrs. Richard Johnston
have the honour of announcing the marriage of their
daughter
Lynn
to
Mr. Wayne Poland
Saturday, the eighth of January
one thousand nine hundred and ninety-four
Fulton, New York

Wedding Announcement from the Bride's and the Groom's Parents—Formal

Mr. and Mrs. Pasquale Altamuro
and
Mr. and Mrs. James Jensen
announce the marriage of
Jessica Lynn Altamuro
and
Eric David Jensen
Friday, the fifteenth of October
one thousand nine hundred and ninety-four

Wedding Announcement from the Bride and Groom—Formal

Mary Anne Smith
and
George James MacLellan
announce their marriage
on Saturday, the twenty-fourth of March
nineteen hundred and ninety-three
Lehigh, Ohio

Birth Announcement—Formal

Although the news of most births is sent via purchased, fill-in announcements, a formal, engraved or printed announcement may be sent instead.

Mr. and Mrs. Steven Cohen
take pleasure in announcing
the birth of a son
Brendan William
on Wednesday, June the twenty-eighth
nineteen hundred ninety-four

INVITATIONS TO DINNER AND REPLIES— INFORMAL

Note of Invitation to Dinner

Dear Jennifer,

John and I would be so pleased if you and Jim could have dinner with us on Wednesday, January the thirteenth, at seven-thirty. It has been much too long since the four of us have been together for an evening, and we have missed you.

We look forward to seeing you.

Yours sincerely,
Amanda Montgomery

Note of Acceptance

Dear Mrs. Montgomery,

Jim and I were so pleased to receive your kind invitation to dinner on the thirteenth.

We have missed seeing you, too, and look forward with pleasure to spending the evening with you.

Sincerely yours,
Jennifer Waite

Note of Invitation to Dinner and the Theater

Dear Mrs. Kemp,

Mr. Forsythe and I would be delighted if you and Mr. Kemp will come to dinner Friday evening, February the twenty-second, at six-thirty, and attend the theater with us afterward.

This is a very early invitation because, if you are able to accept, I will order tickets for the Theater Guild presentation of Hamlet, which, as you know, is extremely popular.

We do hope that you will find it possible to be with us.

Cordially yours,
AnnMarie Forsythe

Note of Regret

Dear Mrs. Forsythe,

Because of the necessity of your ordering theater tickets ahead of time, I wanted to write to you at once that Frank and I must say "no," very regretfully, to your lovely invitation. We would have been so happy to spend the evening with you and Mr. Forsythe, but unfortunately Frank's business travel plans are still uncertain. He may have to be away through the weekend of February twenty-second, and it just wouldn't be fair to delay a definite reply.

Thank you so much for thinking of us.

Cordially,
Judith Kemp

Letter of Invitation to Dinner, to a Good Friend

Dear Amy,

Bill and I just heard from Meg Jordan! She and Peter will be in town the week of November third and want to see all of us. We invited them for dinner the evening of the fifth, about seven o'clock, and hope you and Mike are free that evening to share the happy occasion.

Let us know that you will be coming—it just wouldn't be a true reunion without the two of you!

Love,
Gail

Letter of Acceptance from a Friend

Dear Gail,

Nothing would keep us from accepting your wonderful invitation for the fifth. We did have other plans, but were able to change them so we could all be together.

What a treat it will be for all of us to see Meg and Peter again.

Mike says thank you, too, for arranging what is sure to be a terrific evening. See you then!

Love,
Amy

LUNCHEON AND BRIDGE INVITATIONS, AND REPLIES

Letter of Invitation to a Luncheon

Dear Samantha,

It was great news to hear that you will be spending a month on the Cape, in Chatham. I spent most of my summers there until recently and still have some close friends. With your permission, I would like to write them to let them know you're coming.

In the meantime, I am hoping you will lunch with me on the tenth, at noon, at the Captain and the Admiral. We should have a celebration in honor of your vacation, and I would love to relay to you my knowledge of the area where you'll be staying and to give you some introductions to people I think you'll enjoy.

> Fondly,
> Bridget

Letter of Acceptance

Dear Bridget,

How sweet of you to think of launching my trip to the Cape with a seafood lunch and a travelog from an expert! I hadn't realized that you were practically a Chatham native, and would love to avail myself of your knowledge. I am also grateful for your offer to give me introductions to your Chatham friends. At present, I have no friends there, and it will be reassuring to know they are there.

You are, as always, a most thoughtful and generous friend. I look forward to seeing you on the tenth at noon.

Love,
Samantha

Letter of Acceptance/Regret

Dear Bridget,

There surely is no one more thoughtful than you. I would love to join you for lunch and to hear all about Chatham. I will forego your kind offer to give me introductions to your friends, however. My trip is an attempt to have an unscheduled, unencumbered month, and I fear if I start becoming involved with new friends I won't achieve my purpose. As you know, I've been working around the clock for practically six months and am just plain tired.

I do plan to sightsee and immerse myself in Cape history and attractions, so I especially look forward to our lunch and your advice.

See you on the tenth.

Love,
Samantha

Letter of Invitation to a Card Party

Dear Jasmine,

Dan and I had such a good time at your card party last month that we want to play host and hostess this time. Could you and Wayne come over Monday evening, December the second, about eight-thirty? The Hannigans and the Schiffs will be here, too. You know them, I believe, and they are all excellent bridge players.

The game and the evening would not be complete without you and Wayne. Please say you'll come.

Sincerely,
Sue

Letter of Regret

Dear Sue,

Wayne and I both appreciate your invitation to play bridge at your home on December second. We can't think of a more pleasant way to spend an evening, particularly as we have been taking more lessons and can't wait to try out our new skills. Unfortunately, it will be impossible for us to be there with you. My Aunt Rosamund in Illinois has asked us to visit her that week, beginning the day of your party. I haven't seen her for years, and we have already accepted her invitation. We're both taking part of our vacations at this time and are really looking forward to a rest and change.

We both regret that we can't accept, and we do appreciate your thinking of us. Perhaps, after we return, you'll ask us again.

Cordially,
Jasmine

LETTERS OF INVITATION AND REPLIES FOR WEEKENDS AND ACTIVITIES

For a Weekend Visit

Dear Deirdre and Tom,

October is coming and with it the spectacular view of changing colors from our den window in Vermont. You two have promised for years that you would come for a weekend visit, and this letter is to ask you to set aside the weekend of the third to do just that. We'll be going up on Friday afternoon and hope that you can both get away early on Friday, too, in time to arrive for a late supper, and stay with us through Sunday evening when we have to head back.

This is a casual, corduroy, jeans and sweaters weekend. We've planned nothing but relaxing with two of our favorite friends, so all you need bring are comfortable clothes and shoes (morning walks in the woods are a must!). We would like to take you to dinner at the Inn on Saturday, and that is just as casual as the rest of the weekend, so don't pack anything dressy.

We are so hoping this is the year you can clear your desks and get away—we've missed seeing you and look forward to the chance to spend some "quality" time with the two of you. Please say yes!

                              Love,
                              Sharon

Dear Kate and Reid,

By the middle of July the water temperature should be just right for swimming, and we want you and the children to plan to spend as much of the week of the 14th as possible with us at the Shore. If that is not possible, then at least a long weekend at either end of that week is a must. Brendan and Laura will love the beach, and we've added quite a few new games to our collection, which might keep them amused while we adults catch up on our lives over the past year.

Just let us know when you can come and how long you can stay—and the longer the better, as far as we're concerned! As you may remember from the last time you visited us (and it seems like a hundred years ago, by now) we are completely informal in both schedules and attire. That means sleeping as long as you feel like it in the morning and making plans no more serious than whose turn it is for the hammock in the afternoon. Swimming suits, shorts, and warm sweaters for evening are all you need to bring. Oh yes, we have added bikes to our beach house equipment, so do bring helmets for the children in case they feel like riding, since we have none that will fit them.

Mark and I are so looking forward to your being with us. I've enclosed directions to the house since it's been so long since you've traveled this way. We can't wait to see you all!

Love,

Peggy

Letter of Acceptance

Dear Peggy and Mark,

Your invitation is absolutely irresistible and we would love to visit you at the Shore. Brendan and Laura are practically packed already, they are so excited. You are lovely to invite us for such a long time, and although we are worried you will soon tire of such a noisy bunch invading your tranquility, would be able to come on Friday, the eleventh and stay until Tuesday afternoon. We would arrive around one o'clock on Friday and will have stopped along the way for lunch.

Laura and I plan to bring batches of those chocolate chip cookies we hope you still like, and Reid and Brendan, who have become bread bakers extraordinaire, hope to impress you with their new expertise and will very likely arrive with an armload of French bread. I will call you next week to see what else we can bring that won't interfere with your plans—feeding us is like feeding a small army and we insist on sharing in groceries. And that is a definite. Your generosity is overwhelming, but we simply will not come if we can't share in what it costs to keep us!

We are all so happy about seeing you and thank you for inviting us for what will turn out to be our only real getaway this summer. We have been working around the clock, and the combination of the two of you and the beach sounds simply heavenly. Reid and the children send kisses and hugs, which we shall all deliver in person on the eleventh.

                                    Love,
                                    Kate

Invitation to Extend Hospitality

Dear Cynthia,

We were so happy to hear that you will be returning to Mansfield for a visit and to attend to the final details of selling your parents' house. I'm glad they are happy in North Carolina. They are lucky to have you to take care of the rest of the move for them. We are lucky, too, to have this chance to see you and want you to make us your home base while you are here.

There are many old friends just waiting for a chance to see you again, and Glen and I insist that you make our house your headquarters for your stay. We know you will be frantically busy, but we would like to invite some of your best friends one evening to renew acquaintance. In that way, you won't have to take your brief time running here and there to see them, or be constantly interrupted as they stop by to see you.

Please make us happy by accepting this invitation. We are so sure you will that I am in the midst of getting the guest room ready for you. I'm keeping my fingers crossed for the return mail and the news that you will be staying with us.

> As ever,
> Jennifer

Letter of Acceptance

Dear Jennifer,

Your invitation, with the warmth of friendship that it contained, was one of the most pleasant things that ever came my way. I have been dreading my trip to Mansfield with the thought of all that needs to be done, but such a "welcome home" as yours warms my heart and lightens what I had come to think of as rather a burden.

Of course I accept, and thank you very, very much. I can't tell you how much this means to me. Please thank Glen, too. It will be wonderful to see you both again and to have such an opportunity to catch up and to see other old friends, as well. I am grateful for your arranging to gather everyone together one evening so that I can concentrate on all the details of my trip the rest of the time.

I'll look forward eagerly to seeing you next Sunday.

> Yours affectionately,
> Cynthia

For a Sailing Weekend

Dear Ed,

I know you're as fond of the water and the wide open spaces as I am, so I want you to share them with me over the weekend of August third. You remember that I bought a forty-two foot yawl last spring.

I have her all tuned up and in fine condition, having already spent most of my weekends this summer cruising

aboard her. She handles beautifully, with the best of seago-
ing qualities, and I know you'll enjoy taking your turn at
the wheel. Like you, I don't like using the motor unless the
wind fails.

Tim Kennedy and Roger Imhoff, old cruising mates,
whom you know, will make up the foursome, and you may
be sure that we'll all have a good time. They are coming to
the club with me from the office. If you can meet us at the
4:10 train for Greenwich, Friday afternoon, we'll have dinner at the club and then go aboard. I plan to cruise to the
Thimble Islands and back, if weather permits.

We'll plan to sail back to Greenwich on Sunday, late
afternoon.

I certainly hope to see you aboard.

Yours always,
Marv

Letter of Acceptance

Dear Marv,

It is indeed good of you to include me among your
guests for sailing over the weekend of August third. You
may be sure I'll be on hand and will meet you at the train as
you suggest.

I remember with a great deal of pleasure the many good
times we have had sailing together and, if I'm not mistaken,
Kennedy and Imhoff were with us several years ago when
we sailed from Block Island and were nearly wrecked in that
storm off Nantucket. It will be great to see them again.

Thanks again, Marv, and I'll see you on the third.

As ever,
Ed

Letter of Regret

Dear Marv,

Thanks very much for the invitation to be your guest aboard your new boat over the weekend of August third. You know, better than anyone else, how much I'd like to accept, but I'll have to say no this time.

My dad is coming in from Chicago to be with me from the third until the seventh. I'm more than disappointed not to be with you, and I'd have been delighted to see Kennedy and Imhoff again.

I wish you good breezes and fair weather. Please try me again before the summer slips away. Believe me, I'll do my best to be there.

As always,
Ed

LETTERS OF THANKS

This type of letter should be, at least theoretically, easy to write. When someone has sent you a gift, done you a favor, shown you hospitality, or the like, it ought not to be difficult to express appreciation. The sample letters herewith may be helpful in indicating what else besides a mere "thank you" is properly included in this kind of correspondence.

Just think about what pleasure you would feel to receive a thank you from someone who has taken the time to be expressive about why he or she is thanking you. You would feel your efforts had been appreciated much more to read, "Thank you so much for the exquisite bouquet—the delicate shades of pink and rose look so beautiful in the living room," than to read, "Thank you for the flowers."

The same is true of a letter of thanks for a kindness extended or for a weekend visit. How much warmer "Your thoughtfulness was unending, Sue. We felt as though we were in the lap of luxury in your guest room with the pretty flowers, stack of magazines, and extra down comforter to welcome us after our long drive," sounds than does "Thank you for the weekend. We had a very nice time."

Thank-you letters, if well written, are an excellent opportunity to further strengthen the friendship represented by the occasion, item, or act for which you are expressing gratitude.

FOR WEEKEND AND OTHER VISITS

For Courtesy to Another

Dear Eve,

Your courtesy to my daughter last week, while she was in Los Angeles, was something that I shall never forget. I wanted her to call on you and say hello from me, but your insistence that she be your guest for four days really touched me. You certainly added greatly to the pleasure of her stay in the city.

The dance on Tuesday and the theater party on Thursday were experiences that Linda will remember for a long time. She cannot say enough about you and your friends. I know she has written you her thanks, but I wanted to add my own. I hope that I may have the opportunity some day to return your kindness.

Very sincerely,
Renata West

For *Weekend* *Visit*

Dear Marcia and Craig,

John and I, very simply, had a wonderful time. You are the consummate hosts and we want you to know how special you made us feel. Everything you did for us, from the fresh flowers in our room to the selection of magazines on the night table; from the lovely brunch where we got to meet your new friends to our almost all-nighter talking in front of the fireplace, will long be remembered by us.

After the hectic few months we have been experiencing, your special version of R & R has returned us home refreshed, renewed, and missing you like crazy. Thank you, both, for one of the loveliest weekends we have ever spent.

With love,
Allison

For Dinner

Dear Mr. and Mrs. Winthrop,

Jed and I thank you for including us among your dinner guests Tuesday evening. It was a pleasure for me to meet some of the people with whom Jed works, and I was especially happy to meet both of you.

Your dinner was delicious, and, as one with a beginner's green thumb, it was a real treat for me to be able to tour your beautiful gardens.

Thank you, too, for making two relative newcomers feel so welcome and comfortable. We had a lovely time.

Cordially yours,
Ramona Ross

FOR GIFTS

For Holiday Gifts

Dear Ben,

You couldn't have given me anything that I wanted more or would enjoy more than that handsome desk clock for my office. I remember your pointing out that very clock in the jeweler's window a week ago, and telling me, "You ought to have one of those in your office, Jack. It would add to your prestige." Your beautiful gift will keep me right on time, from now on—and you must drop in soon and see the improvement in my prestige. I want to take you to lunch next week. Can you make it Monday, at one?

Unless I hear to the contrary, I'll expect you then.

As ever,
Jack

Dear Uncle Tim,

You always were my favorite uncle, and the reason is simple—there is no one on earth more thoughtful and generous. If Santa Claus ever were unable to make his rounds on Christmas Eve, I know he wouldn't even be missed if you would consent to step in and take over.

Well, I just don't know how to thank you enough for that beautiful traveling bag, replacing the one I lost during my vacation last summer. It is an exact duplicate—something I thought I'd never have again. Believe me, I am not going to let this one out of my sight. It will be a constant reminder of you and, for that, I'll think all the more of it.

Thank you very, very much.

> With love,
> Rachel

Dearest Claire,

I won't say, "You shouldn't have done it," because that is a worn-out expression, but I will say that you were so generous that you took our breath away, even accustomed as we are to your generosity. All members of the family are enjoying your gifts to the full—Rod, the two children, and I. We all thank you, and they are writing you separately.

My special thanks for the exquisite bracelet. It will remind me of you whenever I wear it, and I assure you I'll not often be without it.

> All my love,
> Betsy

Dear Aunt Polly,

You must be a mind reader, for that writing set that greeted me in the artistic package on Christmas morning was the thing I wanted most of all. I am using it for the first time to write you my heartiest thanks. It seems as if you have a special talent for selecting the gifts people most especially love.

You will be glad to hear that I am to have a full month's vacation next summer, and I am planning to stop off and see you on my way to California, where I shall spend most of my time.

With your present on my desk, I certainly have no excuse for not writing to you often, and to all my friends. You should expect to hear from me frequently!

> Affectionately,
> Judith

Dear Mr. Smith,

Thank you so much for the beautiful leather appointment book. I have already filled in January dates and am feeling very elegant to have such an impressive calendar to carry with me. I very much appreciate working in your department and all the opportunities you have given me this past year to continue to learn and grow. Your gift can only help me become more organized and efficient, and again, I thank you for your thoughtfulness and for your holiday wishes.

Sincerely,
Patricia Lang

For Birthday Presents

Dear Charlie,

I have reached the point where I had decided that I would not make very much of my birthdays, but you evidently do not agree with me. That beautiful watch you sent me reminds me of my birthday, but it does more than that —it reminds me of how much a friend like you means, and always has meant, to me.

I can't tell you how much I appreciate your gift. Thanks, Charlie, more than I can say.

All best wishes for a relaxing vacation—and if you need to know what time it is when you get back, just ask me!

Yours gratefully,
Bob

Dear Aunt Tina and Uncle Jerry,

Mom always tells me that I make more of my birthday than I do of Christmas. Maybe because you knew that, you sent me such a very beautiful gift. Certainly it makes me feel as if it were Christmas. Words can't express how I love the ring, and how much I love you for giving it to me (among other reasons). It just proves again what I've always said—that you are the best aunt and uncle a girl could have.

I understand your next trip will bring you within a few miles of East Lansing. You just have to make time to stop by and see us, so I can thank you in person.

All my love,
Susie

Dear Mom and Dad,

The pictures are being developed and I will send them on as soon as they are returned, so you can see for yourselves how much Danny loves the giraffe you sent in honor of his first birthday. He climbs all over it, pats it on the head, and shares his burgeoning vocabulary with it as he whispers secrets in its ear.

You have made your grandson very, very happy, and I know he sends you one of his loudest kisses as thanks!

Love,
Priscilla

For Wedding Gifts

TO ACQUAINTANCES

My dear Miss Wayland,

The wedding present you sent to Tom and me is one of the most beautiful, as well as one of the most useful, gifts we have received. That lovely flower vase, you may be sure, is going to be much in evidence in our new home. It happens that Tom is a man who is enthusiastic about flowers—and you know what a flower lover I am. You could not have given us a more welcome present.

You must come and see how ideally your gift fits into our surroundings here.

Sincerely yours,
Marjorie Wynne

Dear Mr. Franzen,

It was most thoughtful and generous of you to send us the handsome bridge table and chairs, which will play an important part in our married life. We like them especially because they will be a very pleasant means of having many happy gatherings with friends. Greg joins me in thanking you most heartily for your thought of us.

We are both looking forward to having you as one of our first guests at that table.

Yours gratefully,
Nancy Gallagher

Dear Mrs. Thompson,

Vince and I most sincerely appreciate the beautiful monogrammed crystal goblets from you and Mr. Thompson. Among our gifts was a lace tablecloth with napkins, so you see how well the goblets will grace our dinner table. As you know, we both have many friends and shall be entertaining a great deal. You could not have given us anything we could enjoy more.

When we return from our wedding trip, we hope to have you both dine with us, and we shall drink to your health from those lovely goblets.

Sincerely yours,
Elizabeth Baione

TO FRIENDS

Dear Don,

Your silver candlesticks are perfect, and I really mean just that. The design, the shape—everything about them makes them "a thing of beauty and a joy forever."

You know Rich admits his artistic sense is not all it might be, but you should have been on hand to hear his enthusiastic comments when I opened your box. He joins me in sending you our warmest thanks.

Affectionately,
Mimi

Dearest Gina,

Frank and I were overjoyed with the exquisite coffee service, which now holds a prominent place in our imposing display of wedding gifts. This beautiful remembrance of yours will be used and enjoyed constantly, with many loving thoughts of you.

We are only sorry that you no longer live nearby so that you could run in often and have coffee with us. Thank you again so very much, Gina.

Love,
Leslie

TO RELATIVES

Dearest Nana,

How wonderful you were to start us on our married life with that marvelous set of luggage! When Carl and I are off and away somewhere, as we often will be, it will give us ideas that I'm afraid are going to be hard to live up to. We see ourselves traveling first class, for the best hotels are none too good for that luggage. Certainly it is going to give our departure for our honeymoon a very glamorous start. I think we'll have to take many vacations, too, in order to carry it everywhere we can!

Thanks seem very feeble for such a lovely gift, but we do thank you most sincerely. Your present will remind us of you for many years to come, and we love you very much.

All my love,
Nikki

Dear Aunt Inez and Uncle Rudy,

My favorite aunt and uncle have certainly kept up their reputation for generosity and knowing what is really needed. Nothing could have pleased us more than your beautiful silver carving set. Believe it or not, it matches perfectly the set of flat silver from Frank's parents.

As you know, we love to entertain, and we shall be proud to exhibit and use your gift on many occasions. We hope that one of those will be the first time you dine with us in our new home and see your gift in actual use.

With great love,
Lisa

Dear Uncle Scott,

Brent and I find an ordinary "thank you" entirely inadequate as an acknowledgment of your wonderful wedding gift to us. The check you sent us literally took our breath away. If you only knew how much it means to us, you would be especially happy. As you know, we bought that house on Fenimore Avenue, and so we were going to be economical and not take a wedding trip. But now, thanks to you, we can, and we can also get some very special fittings and furnishings for our new home.

Your sort of kindness and generosity comes once in a

lifetime, and we thank you from the bottom of our hearts. You are going to be our first guest on Fenimore Avenue.

Love,
Kristin

FOR ACTS OF KINDNESS

Dear Chrissy,

When we asked you to take in our mail, we didn't expect you would also take such good care of the garden and check that the windows were closed during that big rain storm you had when we were away. Mr. Hutton and I feel very fortunate that you were watching over the house for us, and thank you, very much, for being so thoughtful and conscientious.

We think you deserve a break after working so hard, so we have enclosed two passes to the movies and some pop-corn and soda money for you and a friend as a little extra "thank you" for all you did.

Fondly,
Mrs. Hutton

Dear Dianne,

Cassie told me you had ordered an extraordinary number of boxes of Girl Scout cookies from her, which has enabled her to win the troop prize. This, on top of your continued patronage of her lemonade stand, your sponsorship of her when she was running to raise money for the Special Olym-pics, and your ongoing friendship to a little girl who is usually very shy about doing these things, is very much appreciated by Andy and me.

Wonderful neighbors are rather a rarity, and we feel especially privileged to be yours, and continually grateful for your kindness to Cassie.

Sincerely,
Jenna Andrews

Dear Mary,

The last month felt like the longest in my life with all the calamities that had befallen us. There was one light at the end of the tunnel, and that light was you. I cannot begin to tell you how much your friendship and your endless thoughtfulness have meant to me. I'm sure I was too tired to be thinking clearly, and each time you appeared—to whisk the children off for an hour so I could rest, or to bring a dinner, or with a pitcher of iced tea—all I knew was that something incredibly wonderful had just happened.

Now that we are back to normal, I know that the incredibly wonderful something was you. There are no adequate words of thanks I can express, but they are now and shall always be in my heart.

All my love,
Deborah

Dear Peggy,

Moving to a new town can be a difficult and sometimes lonely thing to do. Frankly, I was not looking forward to starting over and was uncertain as to how to meet all our new neighbors. The coffee you gave for me took all the anxieties away, and has helped me to feel so welcome on Chestnut Street.

I had a lovely time meeting everyone and you were a wonderful hostess, ensuring that everyone was comfortable and that we had all met and had something to talk about.

Thank you so much, Peggy. I shall never forget your

kindness and thoughtfulness and am so happy to be living across the street from you.

                              Sincerely,
                              Amy Welch

Dear Mr. and Mrs. Small,

    We were frantic when we returned home and couldn't find Max—the boys were in tears and Pat and I were sure he was lost forever. We have had him since he was a puppy and he is an important member of our family.

    Your taking him in and feeding him until we returned from our trip, and continually trying to reach us to let us know that he was safe, were such very kind things to do. We know he would not have survived traffic and other dangers if it weren't for your keeping him safe, and we thank you very, very much.

                              Sincerely,
                              Carol Carlsen

LETTERS TO CLOSE FRIENDS AND FAMILY

If any letters should be spontaneous, informal, and interesting, certainly they should be those to close friends and family. Yet, they often seem hard to write or sound stilted and uninteresting. We cannot tell anyone just what to say in correspondence of this sort, which certainly should reflect the relationship that prompts it. Relax and write as you would talk, about things, events, and people of mutual interest.

The only real "do not's" are such things as do not write at length about people unknown to the recipient of your letter; do not, unless writing to an absolutely intimate friend who serves as a mentor or sounding board, write a litany of woes that only depress the reader; and do not write only a list of questions without also sharing news of your own.

On the other hand, do feel comfortable reflecting, sharing positive news, and simply "chatting" via written word. There are few things in life as enjoyable as sitting down with a newsy, entertaining, spontaneous letter from a good friend or favorite family member. The letter can evoke nostalgic memories, laughter, tears, and a feeling of trust and friendship when it is written with you in mind.

The letters in this section are designed not to tell you what to say, but rather to reflect an appropriate atmosphere and indicate effective language in correspondence with intimate friends and family.

Letters To and From Absent Friends

To a Friend at a Distance

Dear Barbara,

I laughed when I read about Liza's and Kate's increasing confrontations with you—they sounded exactly like what I am going through with Kelly and Allie. Do you think we will make it through their adolescence? We definitely will if we keep on sharing stories so we know we aren't the only ones who are facing these growing pains—theirs and ours!

We continue to muddle along, fighting like crazy one minute and hugging and kissing the next. But there seems to be a ray of sunshine in the horizon—Kelly actually referred to some awful argument we had last year and admitted she had perhaps overreacted. And I had the maturity to say that perhaps we both had done so. You know I could have burst out with raucous laughter, shouting, "Perhaps? Hah! I'll say!"

Other than this situation that we seem to be experiencing in a parallel way on opposite sides of the country, everything else is fine. Work is insane but fun; Rick has been working around the clock himself; and his mother has come for what seems like quite a long visit. I have to keep telling myself that she is the family matriarch and entitled to express her opinion relentlessly, but gee whiz, I don't think I've done that bad a job of keeping things going all this time without benefit of her incessant advice!

I can't wait to hear what you thought about the presidential debate last week. I not only miss you being close by, but I also miss your insider's view of what makes candidates act the way they do.

We are in the midst of taking recycling seriously, at the moment, and it is a lot of work, not to mention the giving up a lot of space for separate containers for each recyclable. Our state hasn't passed laws as strict as those you found when you moved, but we are trying to be responsible and do it ourselves, without having to be told to do so. I think you and the girls were the inspiration when you visited last spring. Kelly and Allie were all ears when you were telling us about it and have become the instigators, and now we're all doing our best to match your efforts.

Must be off to pick up Jamie from football practice. I loved your last letter and can't wait to hear your comments on the debates as well as all your news. Write soon!

Love,
Martha

A Friend's Reply

Dear Martha,

Your letter could not have arrived at a better time—the girls had just finished assuring me that *all* their friends had seen that awful new R-rated movie and that they were the only ones who hadn't, and Teddy was in the throes of an eight-year-old tantrum of his own. I was about to throttle all of them when the mail arrived. A cup of tea and a few minutes with your letter were just what I needed to get a grip!

Work is crazy for me, too—my boss, who has no children and no particular need to get home in a hurry, raises her finely arched eyebrow and glances ever-so-subtly at her watch at 5:30 or 6, when I get ready to leave. It unnerved me at first, but now I just smile and wave a cheery farewell on my way out. After all, I'm in at 8 and she drifts in, dragging her fur coat behind, after 10—so if she wants to make up for a late arrival by staying all night, that's her problem. Tough talk, but you can imagine how hard it is not to start defending myself every time she makes a point of noticing that I'm leaving ahead of her. And I forgot to mention that everyone else clears out as close to 5 as they can!

As to the campaign, we'll have to have a face-to-face debate about who is the best candidate. I'm frankly not sure, at this point, and working in a political office doesn't give me any greater insight than you have from reading the paper and watching the news on television. My instinct is that Belson has the best chance as of now, if Adams doesn't pull a trick out of her hat at the last minute, to win votes.

You'll have to tell me how you feel about Jamie playing

football. I have some concerns about Teddy playing next year on the junior team, and am just not sure what to think.

Bear with Rick's mother. She'll have to go home eventually. You are a terrific wife, mother, executive, houserunner, and organizer. Don't let her make you doubt yourself for a second! And as onerous as she can be, and I remember well from when we all lived closer together, she also doesn't have her own power base anymore, so she has to intrude on yours. Ignore and think other thoughts!

Dance class beckons, and since I am the one with the driver's license, I get to go, too. And then back again to pick up Liza and drop off Kate, and then back to pick up Kate, and so on, and so on, ad infinitum. You appreciate what that is like!

Please write soon—your letters really give me the lift I need. I miss you, Martha! It's very hard to do a sanity check without you here convincing me that if not now, then soon, we'll all get wherever it is we are going without too many head-on collisions.

Love,
Barbara

FAMILY LETTERS

Letter to a Child at Camp

Dear Chris,

Mom and I loved getting your letter. We are so glad that you are having a great time and have so many new friends. We can't wait to see you on horseback and watch the swim meet on parent's weekend, but mostly we can't wait to see you.

You are missing very little at home—Mom has been working practically around the clock on the hospital fund-raising drive for her office and putting in a lot of overtime, and since you've been gone and I last wrote, I have been to Texas, Missouri, and Ontario at area sales meetings. Your sister seems to be having fun at day camp and made you a terrific present in her crafts class, but she misses you a lot, I think. There's nobody around to tease her unmercifully, the way you do, and she has been talking about the "wonderful" day she spent with you at Waterland before you left.

We were very proud to hear about your canoeing trophy and have cleared a place of honor for it on the mantle for when you bring it home.

We are counting the days until we see you, and in the meantime, want to hear more about the Badgers versus the Woodchucks and your new friend, Ian. Write soon, and we will, too.

Love,
Dad

To an Absent Brother

Dear Tom,

We all go back and forth between bursting our buttons at your promotion and amazing new job, and feeling a definite void because you are so far away. But not really so far, I guess—when you were two towns away, we saw each other so infrequently we might as well have been the miles apart that we are now!

There is something wrong that keeps us all staring into our computer screens and apart from each other. Not for long, however—my big news is that John has to head west for a conference, and is taking me with and dropping me at your doorstep on the way. This, of course, presuming you really would be as glad to see me as you said you would! If you meant it, I would be there on the twenty-third and stay through the twenty-fifth. I know you have to be at work, so I thought I could hit your favorite new museums during the day and even volunteer to make dinner for you so we can catch up on all that has happened in the past few months.

Let me know if this is convenient for you. In the meantime, your niece has lost her first tooth and is quite proud, and your dog, both the bane and the joy of our existence, continues to carry your sock around in his mouth. He and Tiger have made friends, and he seems happy enough to be with us, though I think he still is pining for you in his heart. He chewed his way through his gate last week and arrived with a thump and a thud on the bed at about two in the morning. I swear he was laughing with hilarity that he had escaped the kitchen, especially since he now sleeps on the bed with us every night. No more segregation for him! He actually is quite adorable and we are glad to have him, but will of course relinquish him, although not willingly, when you move into an apartment that allows pets.

So let me know if you feel like having a sister invade your life, and tell us more about your job and city living. We love your letters and feel like we know Minneapolis inside and out, just from your descriptions.

Love,
Karen

To Parents at a Distance

Dear Mom and Dad,

You prepared me for most things in life, but you forgot to tell me about the need for a vacation after a birthday party for a five-year-old! It was a smashing success and Tracey loved it, but Chad and I are ready for a warm island, or a long nap, at the least. Enclosed are some of our favorite pictures from the party. Notice the big grin on the birthday girl's face while she's opening your present!

We are counting the days until you arrive—exactly thirty-three from today. Please write to us and let us know what you would like especially to do. We thought we would have a small dinner party a few days after you have had a chance to recuperate from your trip, so that you can meet some of the friends we are always writing about and put faces to names and Tracey is hoping you will want to accompany her to the zoo. She also wants to show you how expert she has become on her bike, and has already put her favorite teddy bear in the guest room so you can "cuddle" it while you are here. We are taking you at your word that you are willing to spend two days with Tracey as your full charge while we are at work. We are taking vacation days for the remainder of your visit, however, because we want special time with you, too!

Chad is off to Chicago tomorrow for a short business trip, and Tracey and I have decided that this is an opportunity for a "girls' " night out and are planning a big night at Casey's Restaurant and the movies.

Chad and Tracey send love to you both, along with mine. And you should be receiving a picture thank-you for that wonderful birthday present very soon.

All my love,
Sherry

LETTERS OF CONGRATULATION

Letters of this type offer a real opportunity to draw friends and relatives closer together, to turn acquaintances into friends, to inject more of friendship into business relationships—in short, to practice that magic human touch that means more in life than most of us realize.

Such letters must, above all, be genuine and sincere. Put yourself in the other person's place. Enter into the pleasure, the pride, and the satisfaction that the particular occasion has given the person to whom you write. Remember also that, to be effective, your letter of congratulation must be written promptly—very soon after the particular occasion.

The letters that follow are meant to exemplify the principle that we have emphasized.

ON SPECIAL HONORS AND ACHIEVEMENTS

My dear Mr. Winthrop:

As a citizen of your town, and one who has its best interests very much at heart, I want to be among the first to congratulate you on your election as Mayor. The large majority given you by the voters proves that there are a great many like myself who definitely wanted our local government to move into the current century and be entrusted to one who is honest, efficient, and loyal to the highest standards.

You may count on me to help in any modest way I can.

Very sincerely yours,
Charles Cernek

Dear Mrs. Espinar,

Only yesterday I saw in the business news that you have been made president of your firm, in whose success you have played such an important part. As one of your former employees, I offer my heartiest congratulations for an honor most highly deserved.

Please accept also my wishes for the very best in your future career.

Sincerely yours,
Polly Roberts

Dear Professor Ladd,

It was a pleasure to hear the radio announcement last night that you have been selected as one of the outstanding scientists of the year, for your work in physics. As one of your old students, I have sometimes thought that if you could teach me, you could achieve anything in your field. And sure enough, here comes this wonderful news!

Seriously, Professor, I can't tell you how delighted I am, and how proud to have had even a humble association with such a distinguished person. Please accept my heartfelt congratulations. I know we shall be hearing much more about you.

> Yours very sincerely,
> Cindy Cortelessa

Dear James,

I knew you would get that well-deserved promotion! I just met Dave Winslow of your staff, and he told me that two days ago you were made advertising manager of the company. Fine work! Also congratulations to the firm. I know that a more able person for the position could not have been selected.

You have my very best wishes for continued and increasing success.

> As ever,
> Mike

Dear Ms McInerney,

Permit me to congratulate you enthusiastically on your speech last night at Milton Hall on "Economic Problems of Today." I traveled a considerable distance to be present, and the effort was well worth while. We hear so many generalities of little value that your presentation was especially welcome and satisfying. I am glad to hear that the speech is to appear in The Economic Review so that more people can benefit from your insights. You may recall that we met last month, in Washington, at the L'Enfant Plaza. I hope we shall meet again soon.

> Sincerely yours,
> Lynn Holton

Dear Judd,

Congratulations on your retirement. There were tears in the eyes of many last night at the dinner held in your honor, for we all know how much we will miss you, as colleagues, and how much the company will miss your good counsel and expertise.

You have surely made more contributions than any other single individual to Consolidated, and should enter your retirement with tremendous satisfaction for all you have accomplished.

May I add my wishes to those of so many others that you thoroughly enjoy your new-found freedom. How wonderful that you will now have time for the countless things that interest you.

It has been an honor and a very real pleasure to work with you all these years.

Sincerely,
Rex Adams

ON A BIRTHDAY

To Friends and Relatives

Dear Non,

Whether you like to remember your birthday or not, I do. In the case of a friend like you, I wouldn't think of letting the occasion go by without special notice. There are many others like me, too, who take a great deal of pleasure in telling you, at least once a year, what an unusually fine person you are. I know this hurts your modesty, but you'll just have to stand it.

In this same mail I'm sending you a little remembrance

which I hope you'll enjoy. Congratulations and best wishes,
Non, and may you have many more anniversaries.

>   Yours,
>   Bob

Dearest Victoria,

It is always a pleasure to say "Many happy returns of the
day" to a person like you.

You know I don't often become sentimental, but on this
occasion I want to assure you that our friendship is one of
the prized possessions in my life, and that I treasure it accordingly. On your birthday I like to think back and enjoy
again the many good times we have had together, and I'm
looking forward to many more.

I hope you received the gift I had sent. I thought it
would go well with that blue dress you bought the last time
we were shopping together.

>   All my love,
>   Maggie

Dear Billy,

Here's a warm birthday greeting to a nephew who
means a lot to me. I can hardly realize that you have
reached your tenth milestone. Why, I can remember
you when you were a tiny baby, and a feisty one, at
that!

It is with great pride that I have followed your record in
school, as well as reports of you from home. Your devotion
and loyalty to your wonderful parents are traits that unfortunately not all children of your age possess. I am sure that
as you grow up you will "go places," and I am going to
enjoy your success with you, all along the way.

Congratulations, Billy, on "Number Ten," and may you

have many more. Watch for the mail. The letter carrier is
bringing you something that I think you'll like.

> Lots of love,
> Uncle Jeff

Dear Sis,

You see, your big brother doesn't forget the birthday of a
very important person. I'm afraid I'm not a very good correspondent, but this occasion I certainly would not pass by.
Many, many happy returns! I wish you would make known
your secret of always staying young!

Do you still enjoy Memphis? It is too bad that you had to
choose a spot so far from home, for we all miss you a great
deal. Here the routine goes along pretty much the same as
usual. Your old friend, Alan Shipman, is getting married
next month. The Andersons are moving to Wyoming—Mr.
Anderson's business, the reason. And the Merriman's cat
had kittens yesterday. I think I've covered the news. Now
let's have some from you.

Please use the enclosed gift certificate for something special—and know that my love is with you.

> Dan

Dear Charlie,

I'm sending this birthday note to reach you, I hope, on
the important day. I'm desolate not to be among your
friends at the party Liz is having in honor of this milestone,
but I'll be with you in thought.

Congratulations and all good wishes. It's the old friends
like you who really count. I don't have to say much more
than that—you know what I mean.

I'll see you soon. My best to Liz, and tell her from me
she's a mighty lucky lady.

> Always,
> Doug

ON GRADUATION

Dear Carol,

As an old friend of yours who enjoyed the thrills of graduating from college some years ago, I want to be among the many who are congratulating you and wishing you the very best from now on. There is nothing else quite like college graduation and the big step out into the world of reality and hard facts, with the challenge that is always waiting there.

You have already shown such marked ability at Harvard that I know there are great things ahead for you. I'm glad you have chosen government as your field. That certainly holds endless possibilities today.

Again, all my good wishes and please keep in touch with me. I know you will have interesting things to report.

Sincerely yours,
David

Dear Bill,

Here's to you! My warmest congratulations on your graduation from Columbia. I'm glad we had two years there together. I have many great recollections of our experience as roommates and of the times we had together. Do you remember the night you were giving an imitation of our chemistry professor, in the lecture hall, and just then he walked in upon us? You turned absolutely purple.

I know the world of teaching will be a little better for your stepping out into it. And I know, too, that in this field, you will make your mark. The profession needs many more like you.

As soon as you know, please tell me where you are going to teach. I want to keep in touch with you.

As ever,
Jerry

Dear Lonna,

I'm sending you, in this very special letter, very special love and congratulations on this very special occasion. You see, everything is very special. And why not? My only niece graduating from high school, and with honors! I think it's wonderful.

You have made a record to be proud of, and, with many others who think highly of you, I'm proud, too. I know you will keep up your fine achievements in the bigger world that's waiting for you. It's good news that you have been accepted at the University of Michigan. You couldn't have chosen a finer college.

Since you'll be traveling a good deal from now on, I'm sending you something to accompany you on your trips. Let me hear from you often.

Yours devotedly,
Uncle Eric

ON RELIGIOUS MILESTONES

Dear Sharon,

Your mother wrote that you received your first Holy Communion two weeks ago, and I wanted you to know how proud of you Uncle Steve and I are. That is quite an important event, and we know how much it means to you. We are having a flower placed on the altar of our church in honor of your first Communion, and hope you will like the little gift we are sending you to commemorate this special time.

Love,
Aunt Laurie

Dear Andrew,

You have no idea how much we wished we could be with you to celebrate your Bar Mitzvah. Your father wrote that you spoke beautifully, and that all your friends were very impressed with your knowledge and sensitivity, and that they had a wonderful time at the party afterward.

Congratulations to you from Mr. Holzer and me. The enclosed is for you, in honor of this important time in your life.

Sincerely,
Mrs. Holzer

Dear Christine,

Aunt Diana and I are so proud of you! We know how hard you have worked toward your confirmation and how much studying and dedication it took, on top of all your school work, to get to this special day.

Your mom wrote that you presented a very beautiful essay during the service, and we would love to see a copy of it, if you would be willing to send it to us.

In the meantime, know you have our love and our continued pride in you and your remarkable efforts.

Love,
Uncle George

ON ANNOUNCEMENT OF ENGAGEMENT

Dearest Susan,

It was so good of you to write me that personal note, telling me of your engagement to Anton Rohrmeier. Congratulations, my dear, to the lucky man, for he has drawn the prize of all prizes in you. I regret that, as yet, I do not know him better, but I certainly intend to, and hope that, in the future, we may become great friends.

All I need to know, dear, is that you've said "yes" to Anton. That, to me, is the best possible evidence that he's a wonderful man. I give you both my blessing and send you my warmest good wishes for a long life of happiness together.

Affectionately yours,
Aunt Loretta

Dear Dennis,

Well, well, well! That's my first reaction to the great news you have just sent me of your engagement to Liz Holly. I am very happy to know you'll have such a lovely woman at your side. There's nobody who deserves the best more than you—and now you certainly have it.

Please give my best wishes to Liz also. You both must have lunch with me some day at the Princeton Club so we can have an official celebration. I'll telephone you soon to set the day.

Always,
Hugh

ON ANNOUNCEMENT OF A MARRIAGE

Dearest Charlotte,

Thank you very, very much for that wonderful letter telling me all about your recent marriage. From all you say, that man of yours must be just about perfect. Or must I make allowance for prejudice on your part? Seriously, I am happier than I can tell you, and I'll always regret that I couldn't be present on the big occasion.

You'll probably not be surprised that I saw it coming. After all, your recent letters contained much between the lines for a friend to read.

My very best wishes to both of you. When you come south next winter, I want you and Sean to stay with me for a good visit.

Affectionately,
Emily

Dear Greg,

It was good of you to send me an announcement of your marriage. I received it yesterday, and I want to send my congratulations and best wishes to you and your bride immediately.

Although I am sorry to say we did not have the opportunity to become very well acquainted before you left our office, I always felt we had much in common and am glad to know of your happiness.

Sincerely yours,
Steve LoCicero

ON A BIRTH

Dearest Kyle,

Your exciting letter arrived this morning, bringing the happy news that your waiting is over and that you now have two men in the family.

It is a lucky baby who has you and Matt as his parents, and Ron and I hope you find every day with little Jimmy a joyous one. As you know, Ron and I attribute a great deal of our happiness to life with the girls and know you'll find the same to be true.

This is a new incentive for us to travel your way in the very near future. Having three of you to visit will be great fun!

Until then, please accept the enclosed with our love and congratulations.

> Affectionately,
> Daryl

Dear Tyler,

How happy I was to receive the good news last night that a baby daughter has arrived and that I am really a great-grandmother! Paul telephoned me from the hospital, which was most considerate of him. He was so much in the clouds and so ecstatic about being a father that I even had to ask him how you were.

Congratulations, my dear child, to you both. I have sent you some of those red roses that were your class flower, and I'll be there myself just as soon as your mother assures me that you are ready to entertain visitors.

> Your loving grandmother,
> Lydia Jenner

Dear Brendan,

Grandpa and I want you to know how proud of you we
are. Mommy told me what a special big brother you are
being to Laura, and we think she is very lucky that she has
you to help take care of her and, when she gets older, to
teach her all the things you know about.

We send you lots of hugs and kisses and this little present, just because it is a very important job to be big
brother!

> Love,
> Grandma

Dear Sue,

Joe and I could not be more delighted! We just received
your birth announcement and assure you that a daughter is
a joy forever. Your little Karen will grow faster than you can
imagine, though, so be sure to treasure every moment and
when you have a chance, send us some pictures of a few of
those moments. We long to be with you and see your little
girl in person, but until that time, a picture would be
lovely.

Joe sends his love, with mine.

> Affectionately,
> Darlene

CONDOLENCE AND SYMPATHY LETTERS AND REPLIES

Letters of condolence are probably the most difficult of all types that one is called upon to write. Only those who have suffered bereavement themselves can completely understand and sympathize in the loss and grief of another. This does not mean, however, that a caring letter of condolence cannot be written by anyone who will apply sincere thought, tact, and understanding to the occasion.

The examples that follow may prove helpful with respect to the kind of thoughts to express, and how to express them.

ON DEATH OF HUSBAND OR WIFE

To Acquaintances

My dear Mrs. Norton,

In this evening's paper I have just read the sad news of your husband's passing. I wish to be among those who are offering sincerest sympathy at this time.

One did not have to know Mr. Norton personally to realize how much he will be missed and mourned in the community for which he did so much.

Very sincerely yours,
Jenna West

Dear Mr. Anderson,

Please accept my most sincere sympathy in the recent bereavement that you have suffered. Your wife will be long remembered by many. She had a rare warmth of personality and beauty of character that left a lasting impression upon all who met her.

Yours very sincerely,
John Corcoran

To Wife of an Employee

My dear Mrs. Vincent,

Our office manager told me this morning of your husband's sudden death. I was deeply shocked, and I want you to know that you have my heartfelt sympathy at this trying time. Earl and I were associated for some time in our work in the office, and I have lost a very good friend.

Please call on me if there is anything I can do.

Sincerely yours,

Lewis Foster

To Friends

Dear Neil,

The extremely sad news of Lucy's death is something that I can still hardly believe. It is impossible to put into words how I feel, but you know the many things I would say. Above all, I want you to know that, as one of your oldest friends, I am with you in spirit, and only regret that distance makes it impossible for me to be with you in person.

My deepest sympathy is with you, Neil.

Sincerely,

Phil

Dearest Lois,

What sad, sad word your letter brought this morning. Your wonderful Norman gone. Words fail at a time like this. If only I could be with you, but you know that I really am, even though there are many miles between us. I believe it does help to hear from close friends and to realize that with their thoughts and prayers they are trying to make your heavy burden lighter, even if only a little.

You know what is in my heart, Lois dear. For your own sake I am not writing a longer letter now, but you will be constantly in my thoughts and prayers.

Lovingly yours,

Marie

Dear Joyce,

You have been in our thoughts and prayers ever since we heard about Ed's death. The loss we feel, too, has so much to do with what a real presence Ed was in our lives—he was friend, confidant, cheerleader, and counselor all in one. He also, with you, shared some of our happiest times and, in fact, helped make them as happy as they were.

We will miss Ed terribly, but shall always be grateful for the friendship he so willingly gave.

Affectionately,
Janice

To a Relative

Dear Aunt Libby,

Mother has just written me of Uncle Walt's death, and I know what a blow you have suffered.

Everyone who knew him at all will have lost a real friend, and for all of us in the family he has left a place that can never be filled. I personally shall always feel that way. You know how much he meant to me. I looked on him as a second father, and I think I never have known a kinder, more considerate person.

Please let me know if there is anything that I can do. I could arrange to be away for a week or two at this time and stay with you, if that would be any help. Please call me if you would like me to do this. In the meantime, you know you have my love and that my memories of Uncle Walt will be with me, always.

Love,
Catherine

ON A CHILD'S DEATH

To Acquaintances

Dear Mr. Bendix,

All in the neighborhood are mourning, and I want to express to you and your wife my deepest sympathy in the tragic death of your little daughter. She was loved by all who knew her, and I know what a tragic sense of loss you are suffering.

I shall call on you personally a little later. In the meantime, let me know if there is anything I can do.

Sincerely yours,
Jules Corday

My dear Mrs. Haynes,

Mr. Morrow and I offer you and Mr. Haynes our most sincere sympathy in your recent loss.

It is, I know, almost impossible to bear, but you are in our prayers and thoughts and those of so many others who share your sorrow.

Very sincerely yours,
Jeannette Morrow

To Friends

Dear Emily,

I feel that anything I can say will be futile at this time. When I heard of little Timmy's death, I was so shocked that

I could not at first believe it. My sympathy goes to you and your husband from the bottom of my heart.

                              Sincerely your friend,
                              Lucy

Dear Tara and Alec,

Llyle and I send you our deepest sympathy. We share your sorrow with you, and know there are no words that can bring you comfort at this time. Tammy's life on earth was all too short, but it was such a happy life because of all the love you gave her.

We feel blessed to have known Tammy for the few years we did, and will always remember her special radiance and the happiness she seemed to carry with her.

Please let us know how we can support you through the coming weeks. We would like so much to do anything that would be of help to you.

                              Affectionately,
                              Grace

Dear Susan and Dick,

We have just heard the very sad and tragic news of your baby's death. It is one of those things impossible to understand, and words are useless at such a time.

Bill and I had to let you know, however, that our hearts ache for you both, and that we want to do anything for you that we can.

May you be given strength to bear your pain and sorrow.

                              With love,
                              Ada

ON DEATH OF FATHER OR MOTHER

To a Relative

Dear Cousin Sally,

I was deeply saddened to hear yesterday of the death of your mother. Unfortunately, I was not privileged to know her personally, but I do know that she had a beauty of character and personality that endeared her to all who came in contact with her. My parents have often spoken of her to me.

Nothing can take from you the wealth of wonderful memories and the happiness that you and your mother shared for so many years.

Affectionately yours,
Jane

To Friends

Dear Les,

The word of your father's sudden death shocked me severely, and I know well what his passing must mean to you. I realize how close you were and that you cherished your special relationship.

I am very glad that I had the pleasure and privilege of knowing him well, for it makes me feel that I can share with you some of the happy memories that will help so much to bring you through these hard days. I know, too, that your faith and courage will bring you peace even in the midst of this great sorrow.

With all my sympathy,
Philip

Dear Josephine,

To think that your mother lived to be ninety-five, and that she passed away so peacefully in her sleep. My childhood associations with her were so close and delightful that I feel unusually close to you at this time.

I remember how she always welcomed me into your home and her unfailing ingenuity in guiding and directing our playtime together. Very vividly I recall the Colonial party she gave for you when you were six years old, and the dolls she dressed in Colonial costume for each of your guests. No child of today enjoys her elaborate birthday affairs as much as we did that simple but clever occasion.

It must be a comfort to you to know that you have cared for her faithfully through these latter years—no daughter was more devoted.

Please call me when you feel up to it so we can talk. In the meantime, anything at all I can do to help you, I would like to do, for your mother was very special to me.

> With loving thoughts,
> Julie

To Acquaintances

Dear Mr. Graham,

Please accept my most since sympathy in the death of your father. I had the privilege of meeting him last month in your office and appreciated his wit and charm. I also observed his fondness for you, which was lovely to see.

I am sorry for the loss you must be feeling.

> Sincerely yours,
> Daniel Forns

My dear Mrs. Sloane,

I wish to express my sympathy in your recent bereavement. I know how much it must have meant to you to have had your mother with you during the last few months. When she took her morning walks she would often pass my house and say such loving things about you. She often confided in me how happy she was to be with you. I hope that the memories of these recent times may make a little easier the sorrow you have to bear.

Very sincerely yours,
Joan Watkins

REPLIES TO CONDOLENCE LETTERS

Formal Acknowledgments

These are often engraved or printed, when it is necessary to answer a large number of notes from those who are not relatives or close friends. When only a commercial card is received, personal notes need not be added. When a personal note has been written on a commercial card, then a personal note from you, added to the printed acknowledgment is proper.

The family of the late
James Willard Norton
gratefully acknowledges
your expression of sympathy

or

Mrs. James Willard Norton and Family
acknowledge with gratitude
your message of sympathy

or

> Mrs. James Willard Norton
> wishes to thank you
> and to express her appreciation
> of your sympathy and kindness

A very brief and formal acknowledgment may be written on a visiting card:

> Thank you very sincerely for your note of sympathy.

or

> Thank you most sincerely for the beautiful roses.

Informal Acknowledgments

> We appreciate sincerely your expression of sympathy and the beautiful peonies that accompanied the note.

or

> My husband and I thank you most sincerely for your kindness in thinking of us and for the beautiful chrysanthemums.

> My dear Mr. Corcoran,
> Thank you very much for your kind note at the time of my recent bereavement. It does make the burden a little lighter to receive such sympathy, and your beautiful tribute to my wife was deeply appreciated. It helps a great deal to know that my wife had so many caring friends and that their friendship is mine at such as time as this.
> > Sincerely yours,
> > William Noland

Dearest Mary,

You will never know how much your wonderful letter meant to me. Norman's death was so sudden and unexpected that I felt stunned and terribly alone. When I heard from you, it was like having you here with me, and I seemed to feel, in a very real way, your love and strength and support. You are indeed a true friend, and I appreciate all that you mean to me, above all at a time like this.

I cannot write more now, but I know you understand. Soon you will hear from me again, and I will let you know all about my plans, which I hope will include a visit with you. It would do me good to be with you.

Affectionately,
Janet

Dear Mr. Hotchkiss,

On behalf of my family, I thank you and the members of the manufacturing department for the beautiful gardenia plant you sent in my mother's memory. Your expressions of sympathy were deeply appreciated, as were your memories of my mother as a member of your department. Her years with Consolidated were very important to her, as were you and her colleagues.

The gardenia is beautifully fragrant, and a lovely reminder—as you know, gardenia's were among mom's favorite flowers.

Thank you, and please thank the others for us.

Sincerely,
Judy Johnston

SYMPATHY NOTES ON OCCASIONS OF ILLNESS OR ACCIDENT

Dear Uncle George,

I was very sorry to hear that you are ill. Please don't misinterpret my saying that it must be pleasant for Aunt Edna to have you around the house. Your business generally monopolizes you, and I know she is enjoying your company. I'm afraid it won't be for long, however, for the reports are that you will soon be returning to your hectic schedule.

I do hope you will be up and about very soon. No one who knows you, with all your pep and energy, can imagine your being laid low for very long. I wish I were near enough to run in and say Hello. Since I'm not, I send you kisses and hugs and all my love.

                                Affectionately,
                                Rebecca

Dear Mim,

It is too bad that you got in the way of one of those germs that have been taking over the town lately. You are so much on the run with your job that I wouldn't have thought any germ could catch you. Don't think for one minute that I am unsympathetic, but the enforced rest may be just what you need to make you let up for a while. You can't do two people's work and not wear yourself out.

Take good care of yourself, Mim, and don't try going back to work too soon. I'll be in to see you when you are feeling a little stronger.

                                Yours,
                                Anne

Dear Louise,

I can't tell you how distressed I am to hear of the automobile accident that has put you in the hospital. I am so thankful that you were not more seriously injured. Bart tells me you are healing nicely and that is good news, indeed!

As soon as you feel up to visitors, I would like to come see you. Until then, rest and feel better.

Love,
Dawn

Dear Jim,

I am extremely sorry to hear that you are in the hospital with pneumonia. I have delayed writing until I knew you were feeling much better. Myrna kept me informed as to your progress, and I am happy to know that the report is excellent now.

The whole department joins me in best wishes for your speedy recovery. Relax, now, and get thoroughly well. Don't worry about your work here. We are managing to get along, and your position is waiting for you whenever you are well enough to join us again. I appreciate all the good work you have done for us.

Sincerely yours,
Leonard Babcock

Part Three

TYPES OF BUSINESS LETTERS

LETTERS OF APPLICATION

A prospective employee may write either of two kinds of letters of application. One is written "blind," not in answer to a help-wanted advertisement, but to some firm with which the individual has decided he or she wants to secure employment. The other is the reply to a help-wanted notice inserted by a firm that desires an employee for a particular position.

In both cases, the object is the same, namely, to sell oneself and one's ability in relation to the position. Too many applicants emphasize how much it would mean to them to get the job. That is the wrong approach.

The emphasis should be placed on how useful the prospective employee could be to the company. This does not mean that bragging is in order, rather that the applicant should present evidence of previous accomplishment, or, if applying for work for the first time, he or she should give the facts as to the background and preparation that would seem to qualify him or her.

A long letter is acceptable only when it is entirely to the point—when every statement is needed to sell the applicant's worth to the prospective employer. In your letter, then, include all significant facts but omit irrelevant remarks and excessive repetition. Put yourself in the busy reader's place. Ask yourself, "What information would I want to obtain about an applicant? What details would I expect concerning the applicant's education and experience?" Above all, be modest, confident, and completely frank. Never conceal vital facts, for an alert employer will promptly detect the omission of such facts.

Such letters are often accompanied by a resume. If this is the case, the letter needn't include as much job history information.

Whenever possible, the name of the person to whom you are writing should be obtained, to avoid having to address the letter "Dear Sir or Madam." When the letter is in response to a newspaper advertisement, it should be addressed as directed, which is often to a box number in care of the newspaper. If this is the case, there is no alternative but to use the salutation "Dear Sir or Madam" or "Gentlemen or Mesdames," which we find preferable to "To Whom It May Concern."

The following examples illustrate the basic principles of good letters of application.

INQUIRIES CONCERNING POSSIBLE POSITIONS
AND REPLIES TO ADVERTISEMENTS

1.

Dear Sir or Madam:

Can you use an employee of good background and education who is capable of performing the following types of work?

1. Proofreading
2. Research
3. Compilation of statistical data

Skills	
and	1. Can compile statistical data.
Abilities	2. Accurate and rapid proofreader.
	3. Can do market and statistical research.
	4. Capable of handling details rapidly and accurately.
	5. Familiar with all branches of music: theory, harmony, counterpoint, composition.

Education: Graduate of New York University, B.A. degree. Completed several courses at Juilliard School of Music. Languages: Have studied Latin, Greek, Lithuanian, French, German.

Present Employment: Am presently employed and have a good record with this company. I wish to make a change because I am extremely interested in the publishing field.

An interview would permit me to elaborate on my

knowledge and experience, and would enable you to determine my suitability to serve your organization.

Yours very truly,
Richard Mahoney

2.

Dear Ms Swenson:

Two weeks ago, I graduated from West High School, and now I wish to secure a position with a firm like yours. Circumstances make it necessary that I begin contributing to the family income as soon as possible, so my intention is to begin my college education slowly, one course at a time, at night. In whatever position I obtain, I shall work hard and faithfully.

Throughout my high school course, I maintained an average of 92.5 percent, and was among ten students awarded special honors in a class of two hundred. During my junior year, I was business manager of the class yearbook, in which capacity I was responsible for the finances. For the first time in three years, the book was a financial success. For the last two years of high school I worked three nights a week and Saturdays in our local drugstore, to supplement my family's income, and I am working now in a temporary position until I can secure a permanent one. Naturally, I am willing to start in a modest way. I want to learn the business and hopefully become eligible for promotion.

I feel that my school years, with their experience both in and out of school, have helped me to develop qualities that would make me useful to you. I can give you excellent references as to my intelligence and dependability from the principal, from my teachers, and from employers for whom I have worked.

I shall appreciate the opportunity of an interview in order to give you more details in which I think you may be interested.

> Very truly yours,
> Anna Heyler

3.

Dear Mr. Reisman:

I am taking the liberty of writing this letter to you, the editor-in-chief, because I believe that you personally may be interested in my services.

I am a graduate of Syracuse University Newhouse School of Communications, rating among the first five of a class numbering one hundred. During my course, I worked for three summers in the production department of Rivers and Company, assisting in various capacities and learning methods and techniques in preparation for an editorial career. In my junior and senior years, I was assistant editor of the college newspaper, *The Daily Orange*.

After graduation, I worked three years for the Benson Publishing Company, in the assistant editor's office. My work comprised editing manuscripts of many different types, helping in the interviewing of prospective authors, conferring with the assistant editor about the acceptance of manuscripts, and doing considerable research and rewriting on some of those that were accepted.

For the last two years, I have been assistant editor at Wesley House. In that capacity, I have handled a great deal of the fiction that the firm has published during the past year. Here, again, I have worked with authors, including much consultation and collaboration while they were writing their manuscripts. This procedure saved the firm con siderable editorial expense after the manuscripts were accepted for publication.

My relations in my present position are mutually pleasant, but I feel I can use my ability to still better advantage.

I should sincerely appreciate the opportunity of an interview at your convenience.

Very truly yours,

John M. Starr

4.

Dear Mr. Carson:

Mrs. Joanne Billingsley, a former employee of your firm, has suggested that I write you about my training and experience, which she believes might qualify me for the position of secretary in your company. I understand that there will be an opportunity for advancement eventually to a supervisory position.

I am a 1992 graduate of Northwestern University, where I specialized in English Literature and Composition. While in college, I attended night school and studied stenography and word processing, with the result that during my last two undergraduate years I served, part time, as secretary to the Dean. I also typed a considerable number of book-length manuscripts for several professors.

For one year after graduation, I studied at the Horton Secretarial School, and during the last three months of that period, at night, I worked with the author, Edith Hemmings, on a manuscript, taking dictation, typing, and even doing some editorial work. I also assisted her with her accounts and her correspondence.

During the past year and one-half, I served as secretary to the director of the Selwyn Foundation. In that capacity, I took dictation, both personal and by tape, handled the director's correspondence, and attended meetings of the trustees, where I took in shorthand the minutes of these conferences, which I later typed and distributed. I was also in charge of the files in the office, and, at the request of the director, I reorganized them on a more efficient basis. In addition to the duties mentioned, I served as receptionist for two hours of each day for two months, as the director wished me to learn also that phase of the office work.

I am leaving this position because my family is moving from this location.

For references, I have an extensive list you may consult, which I will provide for you if you are interested in considering hiring me for your company.

I shall look forward with pleasure to hearing from you, and I hope to be granted an interview. I feel that my training and experience qualify me to give you the high quality of service that your organization requires of its employees. The matter of salary I should prefer to discuss in an interview.

> Very truly yours,
> Elizabeth Downing

5.

Dear Sir or Madam:

In the belief that my qualifications and experience have prepared me for the position of assistant art director of your advertising agency as outlined in your want ad in today's *Clarion*, I enclose my resume for your review. Since it presents my credentials, I shall not repeat them in this letter.

I do, however, desire to call special attention to two

points: (1) I have had the variety of experience that you emphasize as one of the requirements for the position that you wish to fill. (2) The reputation of the firms for which I have worked proves that I am capable of meeting high standards.

May I have an interview at your convenience?

Sincerely yours,

Helen A. Moore

6.

Gentlemen or Mesdames:

In reply to your advertisement in this evening's *Dispatch*, I am applying for the position of typist-supervisor. I believe the following facts show that I could give you services of real value.

I am a graduate of the Katharine Gibbs Secretarial School. As you know, the graduates of this institution receive a thorough grounding in business English and good writing, as well as typing and stenography. I specialized, too, in supervisory and executive courses, at the suggestion of my instructors.

Earlier in my career, I was in charge of the typing department of Whiteley Brothers, responsible for all their correspondence and also for the supervision of twenty data entry clerks. During the year I was there, I increased the production of my department by five percent and received more salary in recognition of this accomplishment.

For the past year I have held a similar position with J.B. Mosley, Inc. Here I have supervised a department of thirty word-processing clerks. I was put in charge of a special training class organized to obtain additional efficiency and succeeded in increasing letter production by ten percent. I have also reorganized and improved the files of the typing department. Mr. Mosley stated that my work was responsible for additional business, and I received another increase in salary.

May I have the privilege of a personal interview?

> Sincerely,
> Martha Knowles

FOLLOWING UP APPLICATIONS

Follow-Up After a Waiting Interval

Dear Mr. Swenson:

About two months ago I submitted an application for a position as product manager in your office. I realize you explained that there were no vacancies at the time, but that you would keep my letter at hand in the event that there might be an opportunity later.

I do not imply, in writing you now, that you would forget me. I just wish to say again that I am certain I could make myself valuable, particularly as, since seeing you, I have recently received recognition for my product development work in the *AMA Journal*. May I ask whether you can foresee a vacancy in the near future?

> Yours truly,
> Andrea Mignone

Follow-Up of Interview

Dear Mr. Hildebrand:

In accordance with your request during our recent interview, I am submitting in writing some of the data in which you were especially interested.

For three years I was a sales clerk at Halley's Supermarket in Cedar Rapids, where I received an increase in salary and special recognition from the management for my knowledge of the stock and efficient service to customers that helped to increase sales by a substantial percentage.

During the past year, I have held the position of sales and stock clerk at the Self Service Mart, in the same city. Here my duties have included assisting customers in various ways in connection with their marketing problems, as well as helping to place and arrange effective floor and counter displays of merchandise. Here also I was in charge of the stock inventory.

With this knowledge and practical experience of inventory, display, and sales, I feel certain that I can prove myself of real value to you.

I hope to hear from you soon.

Sincerely yours,
James Dolce

LETTERS FROM COMPANIES ACKNOWLEDGING APPLICATIONS

Dear Ms Jones:

Your letter applying for a position in sales arrived this morning, and I have read it with more than ordinary interest.

As explained in the advertisement that you answered, we plan to increase our sales staff within the next few weeks. Will you call for an interview on Wednesday, either between 10 and 11 a.m., or between 3 and 5 p.m.? Please ask for me, and bring with you when you come full data on personal background and sales accomplishment.

Very truly yours,
Salvatore Migliaccio

Dear Ms Oglethrope:

This will acknowledge your letter of August 4 applying for a position as secretary with our organization.

Your references and your previous record of work are excellent, and, although I must be frank and say that there is no opening now, I shall be glad to interview you, if you are willing. There is a possibility that there will be a vacancy within the month.

If I do not hear from you to the contrary, I shall expect you Thursday, August 6th, at 9:30 a.m.

Yours very truly,
Jean Carlsen

Dear Mr. Corcoran,

Your letter of February 22, in which you apply for a position as bookkeeper, has just come to my attention.

Unfortunately, there is no opportunity at the moment, but I definitely will keep your application in our active files, for I am very well impressed with both your personal and your business qualifications. I suggest that you get in touch with me again in six weeks if you are still interested.

                        Sincerely yours,
                        Scott Aabel

Replies to Acknowledgments of Applications

Dear Ms Whitby:

Thank you for your letter acknowledging my application of June 14 for a position in word processing with your firm. I note that you say that within a week a temporary place may be open during the vacation of one of your regular word processors.

I shall appreciate your informing me as to the exact time, for I shall be glad to fill the vacancy, in order to prove my ability and in the hope that the temporary assignment may lead to permanent work.

                        Very truly yours,
                        Louise Nelson

Dear Mr. Barron,

Your courtesy in acknowledging my recent application in regard to the opening for a bookkeeper is much appreciated. I am pleased to hear that within a short time you will need additional assistance and that I may depend upon your letting me know when that time comes.

I feel sure that I can turn my previous experience to good

account on your behalf, and I assure you that I will spare no effort to prove my worth.

> Sincerely yours,
> Frederick Wolgast

LETTER OF INTRODUCTION

Dear Peter,

Kristoffer Roggemann, a young friend of the family, the bearer of this note, will highly appreciate, as shall I, your giving him a few minutes of your busy time.

He would like to talk with you about the possibility of an opening in your copywriting department. In addition to his excellent specialized education, he has already done successful work in copywriting and layout for direct mail advertising. I believe he shows real promise, and I think you will agree with me.

Thank you, Peter, for your courtesy.

> Sincerely,
> Diana

FOLLOW-UP OF REFERENCES FOR INFORMATION ABOUT APPLICANTS, AND REPLIES

Dear Mr. Poland,

Your name is among several references given by Mr. Denis Rinello, who wishes us to consider him as a possible office manager with our firm.

We shall appreciate your giving us your opinion of Mr. Rinello's character, personality, intelligence, habits and—very important—his success in his personal relationships with other people. We want a person with originality of ideas and a real capacity for hard work, too. I know that your comments will be valuable, and please make them entirely frank. Anything you have to say will be treated as strictly confidential.

Thank you for your cooperation.

Sincerely yours,
William Benson

Dear Ms Wiley:

Karen Clark has applied for a position with our organization as receptionist, and has given your name as a reference. We shall appreciate hearing from you.

Of course, you know the importance, to us and to the applicant, of your giving a perfectly frank opinion of her and of the qualifications that she may possess for the job in question. We should particularly like to have your estimate of her personality and her ability to meet people courteously and graciously.

Strict confidence will be observed concerning what you tell us. Thank you for your assistance.

Yours sincerely,
Amelia Coppola

Dear Mr. Matteis:

I take genuine pleasure in recommending Mr. Louis Mattutini as office manager in your organization.

For many years I have known him personally, as well as his family, and during his five years in business I have followed his progress with much interest. He is a young man of education, high ideals, and sound integrity. His originality of ideas and capacity for hard work have been outstanding characteristics ever since his high school days. So far as I am concerned, you may tell him what I have said—I've often told him so myself.

I honestly believe that your firm would be fortunate in obtaining his services.

Sincerely yours,
Joseph Soury

Dear Ms Budding:

It gives me real satisfaction to answer your note concerning Robin Dawson.

She worked in the same office with me for two years as an editorial assistant and was one of the best-liked employees in the company. Several times she took my place as managing editor and showed a marked talent for handling problems that arose. Ms Dawson is a graduate of Connecticut College, where she maintained an enviable scholastic record. I cannot speak too highly of her.

I am convinced that she would bring credit to you and your organization.

Yours very sincerely,
Margaret Vose

LETTERS OF INQUIRY

Letters of inquiry are written to obtain information of one kind or another. The writer (a) may have decided that he wants data on some subject and may communicate with some source from which he or she believes it can be obtained, or (b) he or she may write in response to an advertisement, to learn more than it tells.

Especially in the first instance, the letter should be very clear and explicit in order that the recipient may know exactly how to comply with the request.

REQUESTS FOR INFORMATION, WITH REPLIES

1.

Gentlemen or Mesdames:

   I plan to leave New York in three weeks, on August 7, and travel by train to San Francisco, taking a rather extended vacation en route. Since I am not sure how to do the planning, I would appreciate the cooperation of your Bureau. Please bear in mind the facts set forth below. Accommodations are to be first class.

   It is my intention to spend four days in Chicago, and I wish to stay near the theater district. From there, I shall go to Denver and stay one week, visiting the principal points of interest in and around the city. If a trip to Pike's Peak from Denver is feasible, I wish to include that. My next stop will be Yellowstone National Park, where a horseback tour of the park is to be included. After that, the Grand Canyon of Arizona, with the regular sightseeing trip, and Salt Lake City including the Great Salt Lake.

   Kindly inform me when you have completed the arrangements and I will call at your office to go over them with you.

Very truly yours,
Robert F. Armao

Dear Mr. Armao,

   This is to acknowledge your letter of July 25, entrusting us with the planning of your vacation trip. Thank you very much for your patronage.

   You may rest assured that we will spare no effort to plan

a trip that will meet your every requirement, and which will give you the pleasure and recreation that you desire.

As requested, we will inform you when the arrangements are completed, at which time you can call and approve them.

> Yours very truly,
> Nelson Rockman

2.

Dear Sir or Madame:

Will you please send me information on your grounds service for suburban residences? If it is what I need and want, and is satisfactory as to price, I shall be glad to subscribe to it. I might wish partial, or perhaps complete, service.

I have a ten-room house, situated on two acres of ground. There is a privet hedge extending for some one hundred and fifty feet along the front; two flower gardens, approximately 60 by 15 feet, in the rear; and two large lawns to be kept weeded and mowed. There are also a considerable number of shrubs and a grape arbor that require pruning. Will you kindly let me know, too, if your service is year-round, including leaf removal and shoveling of walks and driveways after winter storms?

I shall appreciate hearing from you as soon as possible.

> Yours truly,
> W. Robert Connor

Dear Mr. Connor:

We thank you for your letter of February 4, inquiring about our grounds service for suburban residences.

Enclosed is a booklet we have prepared especially to answer just such inquiries as yours. You will note that our service varies according to how much the householder wishes to have done. For example, sometimes the gentleman or the lady of the house prefers to care for the flower gardens; and some prefer to mow their own lawns.

Our service is complete, and all year-round. We keep hedges trimmed, mow lawns weekly and keep them in healthy condition, give flower gardens the best of care and cultivation, take care of all necessary pruning, rake leaves in the fall—and yes, we do keep your walks, driveways, and porches free of snow and ice during the winter.

The enclosed booklet gives you full details, with our rates. May we suggest, however, that you call and ask one of our representatives to inspect your property at your convenience. Such a procedure is likely to result in an arrangement most economical and satisfactory to you.

Thank you for your interest, and we shall expect to hear from you again soon.

Sincerely,
Davidson Gordon

RESPONSES TO ADVERTISEMENTS

1.

Dear Sir or Madam:

Please send me by return mail, as advertised in the *Challenge* of March 3, your course on "How to Make Money by Writing." It is understood that this course may be examined for five days and then returned, with no obligation, if I do not wish to keep it.

Very truly yours,
Elizabeth Johnston

2.

Dear Sir or Madame:

I am interested in the Wilmington residence that you are advertising for sale, but I should appreciate a few details in relation to my particular family and present circumstances.

A. Is there a good shopping and marketing district within walking distance?
B. Is the immediate neighborhood free from heavy traffic as a menace to small children?
C. Does the house need any substantial amount of redecoration?
D. Is there any finished bedroom with bath, on the third floor?

A prompt reply will be appreciated, as I am seriously considering relocating to Wilmington and this house sounds ideal for my purposes.

Sincerely,
Gary Kauffman

CLAIM AND COMPLAINT LETTERS

Letters of claim and complaint should not be difficult to write. They are based on facts, if there are really good grounds for the claim or complaint, and it is a question of presenting these facts clearly, concisely, and forcefully. One warning is in order: If you want your letter to be effective, you must know the facts—not just generalize and jump to the conclusion that the other person or organization is wrong. Sometimes there are the well-known "extenuating circumstances" that make the other side of the case reasonable, too.

CONCERNING DEFECTIVE MERCHANDISE, AND REPLY

1.

Dear Mesdames or Gentlemen:

One week ago, April 2, I ordered fifty lamp shades, my order No. 2545, and your invoice No. 67563. The shipment arrived yesterday, presumably in fulfillment of my specifications.

The entire lot is unsatisfactory. The color is not as specified, the material is of inferior quality, and the shades are not even all of the same size. Some of them also have defects that are glaringly visible.

I am returning the entire order by express, collect, and shall expect to receive the correct merchandise at the earliest date possible.

> Very truly yours,
> James Culyer

2.

Dear Service Manager:

Five days ago I was in your house furnishings department and was attracted by your special display of floor tiles. The clerk showed me several varieties, and one of them, in the size and pattern that I eventually selected, showed wear and several defects in the material.

Naturally, I supposed that this was simply a display item,

and it did not occur to me to call the clerk's special attention to the conditions I have described. Imagine my astonishment and disappointment, when my tiles arrived yesterday, to find that I had apparently received the defective ones. I can see no excuse whatever for this whole discreditable business.

I always try to be a reasonable person, and I am willing to listen to an explanation, if you have one. In the meantime, of course, I expect you to send for and replace the defective goods.

Yours truly,
Barbara Anselmi

Dear Mrs. Anselmi:

Thank you very much for telling us about your unfortunate experience with our house furnishings department. You have done us a favor in bringing this matter promptly to our attention.

The whole matter was badly handled, so we are not going to try to make excuses.

We are sending immediately for the defective merchandise, and we shall see that your order is filled in a satisfactory manner. In fact, I am giving it my personal attention.

Please accept our apologies for the inconvenience caused you.

Sincerely yours,
Sherri Adams

Letter Regarding Delay in Shipment

Reporting Delay

Dear Mr. Morganti:

You have generally given us such excellent service that we regret having to call your immediate attention to Purchase Order No. 3254, placed with you, under date of June 14. It should have reached us two days ago, and it still is not here.

Perhaps this shipment is en route now. In any event, we shall appreciate your telephoning us and letting us know exactly how matters stand. If the order is not on its way, please take immediate steps to send it, and mark it Priority Mail. In case you cannot furnish all items now, please ship the men's shaving kits at once.

We shall expect your telephone call upon receipt of this letter.

> Yours truly,
> Stephen Feeney

Acknowledgment of Delay Report

Dear Mr. Feeney:

This is to confirm our telephone conversation, according to your request. We would willingly take the blame if it were ours, but we have checked thoroughly on the delay in delivery of your order, and have found that everything was promptly and efficiently taken care of at this end. The order was correctly filed, carefully packed, and promptly shipped on June 16, via Trans-State Trucking.

We have already reported your complaint to that service, and a tracer is now out. In the meantime, however, we have made up a duplicate of your order and it is already on its way to you by special truck, at our expense. We fail to understand how this trouble occurred, and, as you see, we have done our best to correct matters, for we value you as one of our most highly esteemed customers.

Thank you for letting us know at once about the delay, and we trust that you will receive that duplicate shipment promptly. This letter will confirm our telephone conversation of this morning.

Yours very truly,
Angelo Morganti

LETTERS REGARDING REFUNDS

Letter Refusing Refund

Dear Susan Clark:

We have received the blouse that you returned and, with it, your letter requesting credit in full ($42.95) for the merchandise.

It is our aim, as you know, to maintain a generous credit policy, but we are sure you will understand that we have to protect all our customers, and that therefore we cannot accept returned goods that have been worn. Unfortunately, the blouse that you purchased has obviously been worn. Undoubtedly, you simply did not realize the point of view which we have explained.

Since we cannot resell this blouse, we are regretfully unable to credit your account in this instance, even though we certainly value your continued patronage highly and should like to please you.

The blouse is being returned to you by our afternoon delivery. We hope we may serve you in the future.

> Yours very truly,
> John Boas

Letter Granting Refund

Dear Ms Montgomery:

In your letter, just received, you call our attention to our guarantee of "Satisfaction or Money Refunded." We note that you have returned the merchandise purchased two days ago, because a mistake was made by one of our clerks and you received the wrong goods. We always live up to our promise to customers and are therefore enclosing a check for the full amount of your purchase.

We really do not make many errors such as this, Ms Montgomery, and we take pride in that fact. We value your patronage, so won't you drop in again soon and permit us to see that this time you get exactly what you select?

> Sincerely yours,
> Brian Maday

Letters Regarding Complaint and Redress

Letter Regarding Bad Check

Dear Miss Morrello:

I am sorry to have to inform you that your check bearing the date of December 20, drawn to me in the amount of $150 for purchases at our boutique, has been returned.

On December 21, I deposited the check in the Smithtown Trust Company. I received it back this morning with the notation "Insufficient Funds." We all make mistakes, at times, in the matter of our bank accounts, and I am sure that this is what happened in your case, perhaps because of heavy purchases for the Christmas season.

Of course, you understand my position in wishing to have the error corrected at once. Will you therefore please send me immediately a certified check for $150 plus bank fees (statement enclosed) which I was required to pay. Your prompt attention will enable me to adjust my account with the bank and to return your original check.

Yours very truly,
James Godfrey

Complaint Regarding Redress or Adjustment

Dear Building Manager:

Yesterday, owing to your carelessness, I had a very painful accident in front of your building. Serious as it was, my physician informs me that he cannot yet tell what the full consequences will be.

While I was walking along the sidewalk on the south side of 112 Judson Street, my heel struck your sidewalk grate, which was not fastened from below, and which flew up to a perpendicular position so that I plunged violently downward, waist-deep, sustaining bruises, abrasions, and severe shock.

My brief case, which I was carrying at the time, was hurled from my hand, scattering valuable original papers in the street, where many of them were damaged so badly that I shall have to go to the expense of having new documents drawn. In fact, one paper, which will require research to duplicate, was carried away by the high wind that was blowing and I never did recover it.

Your carelessness in permitting the condition described to exist was inexcusable. I shall expect to hear from you immediately as to what you intend to do in this matter.

Yours very truly,
Richard Grossman

Company's Reply to Complaint

Dear Mr. Grossman:

Your letter describing your accident in front of 112 Judson Street arrived this afternoon.

We exceedingly regret the fact that you suffered such an experience, and we have already made an investigation on the premises. Recently we have had some trouble with the custodian in regard to certain aspects of safety around the building. He had improved lately, as a result of our careful check upon him, and we had hoped that all was well. This is the only incident of the kind that has ever occurred under our management, and we regret it as much as you do.

Our legal representative will telephone you tomorrow for an appointment to discuss the entire matter. You may rest assured that we wish to arrange a settlement that will be entirely satisfactory to you.

Yours very truly,
Arthur Bisbee

Customer's Letter Threatening Legal Action

Gentlemen:

The matter of the bad paint has reached the point where it would be funny if it were not so serious. Another week has passed since I wrote you my second letter—a total of three weeks since you evidenced such a promising reaction to my original letter of complaint. Still no results.

You certainly cannot possibly think that I have been either unreasonable or impatient. I want action within three days of the date of this letter or I will place the whole affair in the hands of my attorney.

Sincerely,
Richard Amberg

SALES LETTERS

Sales letters, obviously, are meant to sell something. Yet, too often they are stilted and mechanical, lacking in interest to the prospect. A reader will not act unless and until you have made him want what you are trying to sell, and, to do that, you must stimulate his interest.

The time-honored formula cannot be improved: attention, interest, desire, action. It is the function of the beginning and of the end of your letter to get attention and action; the body of the letter must cultivate interest and a real desire for your product or service. But care should be exercised not to write too much. The sales letter should be natural, sincere, and convincing.

Write while the iron of your imagination is hot—but it is wise to lay your completed work aside and let it cool a bit. Read it, aloud, a little later. If it still sounds effective, send it.

Letters Soliciting New Accounts

1.

Special Allowance for January Promotion of How-To and Self-Improvement Books!

Are you looking for an easy way to increase your sales? Why not let the "Everyday Handbook Series" do the trick? We feel so strongly about the year-round sales potential of these popular little books that we will cooperate with you and offer this series for the month of January with a special allowance for your advertising and promotion.

Certainly you don't have to be told of the perennial demand for "how-to" books. The "Everyday Handbook Series" supplies this demand admirably because it offers practical information for self-improvement in workaday activities in business as well as during leisure hours. These up-to-the-minute digests are on a wide variety of subjects, simplified for home use. Each handbook is an authoritative yet "popular" presentation suitable for any reader's permanent reference library.

Display the "Everyday Handbook Series" prominently in your store, and you will be amazed how fast these books sell. Your customers will buy them almost as freely as they would buy magazines, because "Everyday Handbooks" provide the alert home owner with basic information in convenient form and at just the right price.

If you would like some of the enclosed "Everyday Handbook Series" brochures imprinted for your own use, we will be pleased to supply them—in proportion to your January stock order. Counter racks are also available. Fax, write, or call for details.

Get your year's business off to a good start with the "Everyday Handbook Series." See the convenient order form enclosed. Order now to obtain the special allowance.

Very truly yours,
Holliwell Press

2.

Dear Mrs. Whitman:

"The patter of little feet"—a phrase with very sentimental association—but not where mice are concerned.

If in your home there are little feet pattering about that don't belong there, call us at once. We get rid of mice, rats, and other undesirables. Our exterminating service is complete, effective, reasonably priced, and guaranteed as to results. Our employees are quiet, courteous, and efficient. They leave no dirt anywhere. They do not wear uniforms, and our cars carry no advertising on them.

The exact price of a particular service depends, of course, on just how much is to be done. We can refer you to many customers who will recommend both our work and our prices.

Call 834-4978 now, and one of our experts will come immediately.

Silvia Barrett
President

3.

Dear Mr. Abercrombie:

William Best has suggested that we send you some of the highlights of his latest book, *How to Write What Will Sell*. It has itself been a best-seller in its field ever since publication, and we are glad to do as he suggests.

The enclosed leaflet you will find fascinating reading, but it does not begin to be as informative and interesting as the book. Mr. Best, in his newest publication, has gathered together and made available his many years of experience as a successful writer of both fiction and nonfiction.

He tells you how to build plots and create lifelike characters, explains how and where to get material for articles of all kinds, and gives a list of the best markets, with details as to content wanted and rates of payment.

The book is invaluable both for the person who plans to make writing a career and for the individual who would like to earn extra money through part-time writing.

We want you to see this book. If you are not certain that it is worth to you much more than the moderate price of $19.95, you may return it, with no obligation.

Don't miss this rare opportunity. Mail the enclosed card NOW!

>   Very truly yours,
>   Charles B. Singer

4.

Dear Mr. Vines:

Only a real artist can paint a picture.

Oh, yes, any one can mix colors together, put them down on canvas, and call the result a picture—but what a difference!

Undoubtedly, you recognize the analogy with respect to letterheads. Some are just letterheads. Others are works of art. Our pride in being artists in this field is justified by our experience with many well-satisfied customers. We do more than print letterheads. We plan, design, and execute them in such a way that the result does the most credit to your firm. It enhances your reputation and helps to bring in additional business.

Mail us a letterhead of yours now, and we will give you, with no obligation, expert advice as to how we can redesign and print it to make it more effective for your purpose.

> Yours truly,
> Howard Carter
> Elite Printers

5.

Dear Amanda,

Welcome to West Haven!

We know you're most welcome of all to your mommy and daddy and to your little brother, who arrived only one year ago. What good times you're going to have together!

You're going to like West Haven—we're sure of that—and we're sure our lovely town is going to like you.

This letter is to tell you that we have a big store with many pretty things for little girls. There is a special floor set aside for what you may need now, and as you grow older. We have all kinds of nursery equipment—cribs, bassinets, baby carriages—and wearing apparel for indoors and outdoors. One special item we recommend is our novel snuggle-blanket with a zipper, so that you can never get uncovered on a cold winter's night.

Please congratulate your parents on your arrival.

Show this "welcome note" to your mommy and tell her to call us up right away and let us know what you need. We'll have it there before you can say "baby bunting."

Your new friends at Wilson, Merrill & Company

6.

Dear Mr. Bellamy:

We know you're busy, Mr. Bellamy, and that is why we're writing you. It's just because you're busy that we want to save your time when you plan that well-earned vacation trip.

Too often you work so hard, planning, that the actual vacation is not half the fun it should be. You go around from office to office and perhaps write a score of letters to get assistance. Perhaps some of the letters aren't even answered.

Travel Anywhere saves you that kind of fuss and fret and frustration. As expert professionals in travel, we find, plan, and arrange the trip you want, for what you want to pay. Our facilities, consolidated in one office, cover every phase and kind of travel, and we are authorized representatives of all resorts, tour operators, and transportation companies.

Our advice is free. Our fees are moderate. Our results are highly satisfactory. Our many enthusiastic customers are our best recommendation.

We can help you. Drop in soon, or call 967-6100.

Very truly yours,
Janice Baragwanath
Travel Anywhere

7.

Dear Ms Keith:

In your particular work, you are an expert. As such, you know the value of consulting with other experts, in order to benefit from their knowledge and suggestions.

Suppose that you had available, and at a very moderate fee, a group of experts in the field of business, economics, finance, and government with whom you could consult at any time.

Suppose, too, that each of these experts continually studied and analyzed every authoritative source at his or her command and, besides that, traveled both here and abroad to get first-hand information, trends, and reactions.

Then suppose that this remarkable group sent you, every week, a clear, comprehensive, joint report for your personal use and application. You would gladly pay $24.00 a year for their services, wouldn't you? You get all this in *World Survey*, the new magazine for business people that is on the newsstands this week, for its first appearance. You cannot afford to be without it.

If you act now, the enclosed card entitles you to a forty

percent discount on one year's subscription. This offer is good for a limited time only. Send in the card TODAY!

The Editors
World Survey

SPECIAL LETTERS TO LONG-TIME CUSTOMERS

1.

Dear Mr. Bradford:

This is a special letter to you as one of our valued dealer-customers.

Because of the steady pressure of costs, we shall regretfully be obliged to advance by ten percent our entire line of pen-and-pencil sets, beginning the first of this coming month. Even at some loss to ourselves, we have postponed taking this step until the last possible moment.

Of course our sales department will send you an official notice within a day or two, but we feel that there are certain especially good business friends—you among them—who deserve this preliminary notification.

As you know, we do not carry a very large stock, so act now and place your order while you can still benefit from this special opportunity.

Yours truly,
Walter R. Kennedy

2.

Dear Miss Horowitz:

This coming month we are featuring a special sale of silk dresses of such outstanding value that we want to let you, as one of our good charge customers, know in advance about it.

We invite you to attend a preview of this line, from 10 a.m. to 4 p.m., Wednesday, March 8, the day before it is put on sale to the general public. The dresses to be shown are of exceptionally fine fabric and design and are offered at attractively low prices, especially considering conditions today. Materials include colorful shantungs, pongees, and silk crepes and chiffons.

Bring this letter with you to the fifth floor and present it to our Miss Benjamin, who will be glad to give you her personal attention. She will be expecting you.

                              Cordially yours,
                              Susan Friesell

P.S. You may find it a convenience to lunch at our new
     restaurant just opened on the tenth floor.

3.

Dear Customer:

This is our Tenth Anniversary—but you are having the party!

After all, that's absolutely appropriate, for it's you, and other good and loyal customers like you, who, by their generous and continual patronage, have made our mail-order business flourish, so that each of our anniversaries has been bigger and better.

All our patrons, long-time and new, can enjoy the party for the next two weeks. And it will really be a party—with a dozen great bargains for you and hundreds of other friends.

The enclosed catalog, which can be used for your orders, gives you an idea of what is in store for you. Note, for instance, how we have slashed the prices on rainwear and outdoor accessories; three-year-guaranteed stainless-steel cutlery; long-wearing patio furniture covers; and other items.

Look over the enclosed catalog and select the articles that you want and need. We may not be able to offer you these wonderfully low anniversary prices again—these phenomenal savings for you, your family, your home.

You have a week's trial, free, of any starred article you may select. Merchandise is prepaid to your door. If you're not entirely satisfied, return the goods, and owe us nothing.

This opportunity may not occur again. Mail us your order immediately and we will fulfill it and have it to you by return mail, while inventory lasts.

> Yours for anniversary savings,
> George E. Hastings
> President

LETTERS TO REVIVE INACTIVE CUSTOMERS

1.

Dear Ms O'Donnell:

Our business has been excellent lately—many old customers have been generous with their orders; and we have been unusually fortunate in adding a considerable number of new accounts. But we want you to know that not even this state of affairs satisfies us.

We are disturbed about you. Until three months ago, of all our customers you were one of the best, in every sense of the word. Apparently, you have decided to discontinue your patronage. If you were in our place, wouldn't you be puzzled and disappointed?

If you consider us to blame in any way—if there is anything we have done, or have not done, that has alienated you—please let us know and give us a chance to make things right.

Having expanded our premises and added to our staff and our stock within the last month, we are in a position to give you even better service than before—and we want you to be among those whom we are serving this spring with our full and modern line of household appliances.

Please let us hear from you soon.

> Yours very truly,
> Eileen M. Kelly

2.

Dear Mr. Rinehart:

A while ago, an old friend of mine suddenly just "disappeared"—discontinued his friendly calls, and seemed to want to avoid me when our paths crossed. I don't believe in letting matters rest like that, so I called him and asked him what was the matter.

It proved that, quite unintentionally, I had hurt him by something I had said—and I immediately cleared up the misunderstanding.

For four months now, you have placed no order with

me, whereas we used to have a mutually pleasant and profitable relationship. Am I unconsciously responsible for something said or done that displeased or offended you?

I value your business highly, but even more your good will. So won't you tell me if anything is troubling you that is within my power to adjust? Don't bother to write. Just call me on the phone and let's have a friendly chat.

Cordially yours,
Paul B. Winslow

LETTERS INTRODUCING SALES PEOPLE

1.

Dear Ms Winters:

You have for a long while been a very good customer, and always gave our salesman, Arthur Merriwell, a most hospitable reception. We sincerely regret to inform you that Arthur died suddenly a week ago.

This is a special note to let you know that Dawn Mittick is taking over Arthur's territory, and that she will be calling on you soon. We think a lot of Dawn and of her business knowledge and efficiency, and she knows Schwab Hardware from A to Z.

We are sure that you will enjoy with Dawn the same friendly and profitable relationship that you knew with Arthur.

Cordially yours,
Cheryl Flood

2.

Dear Ms Citron:

   You will probably regret as much as we do that Bill Hilliard, who represented us so well and for so long, has been obliged to move west for his health. However, Austin Bradley, who for a long while has handled our office work on your orders, is glad of the opportunity to go into the field, and especially glad that you will be among those whom he will serve.

   We are sure that our mutually pleasant relations will continue when Austin takes over your area, for we know he will serve you well and that you will like him personally. He will be calling you for an appointment soon. Thank you again for your many years of loyal patronage. We shall spare no effort to prove worthy of its continuance.

                                   Sincerely,
                                   Elizabeth Hiemstra

ORDER LETTERS

While at first order letters might seem to be nothing but purely a routine affair, it is worth noting that they can be made more than that. In other words, whether it is a case of placing an order or acknowledging one, a touch of courtesy and friendliness always helps to form a new business relationship or cement an old one. This principle holds especially true when any misunderstanding is to be cleared up.

Of course, clarity is absolutely essential. It prevents misinterpretation, delay, and sometimes consequent friction and unpleasantness. In all letters concerning orders, then, remember courtesy and clarity. They will go far toward making your order letters a success.

LETTERS ORDERING GOODS

Letter Ordering from a Catalog

Dear Order Processing Manager:

Please send me by express mail the following saws and blades as listed in your July 23, 1993 catalog:

1 for cordwood and felling	24 Λ 1328	$ 8.75
1 for heavy use	24 A 1319	$ 7.65
1 for pruning and firewood	24 A 1327	$ 8.15
1 special-duty pruning saw	7 A 823	$ 9.72
2 Replacement blades	2 A 1317	$ 2.55
		$36.82

Enclosed is my check for the merchandise, plus $10.90 express mail shipping charges and $2.95 tax, for a total of $50.67. I shall appreciate your giving this order your prompt attention.

Yours very truly,
Ward Riley

Letter Ordering from an Advertisement

Dear Sir or Madame:

Will you kindly send me two of the cellular phones, order number 2c321, as advertised in the "Daily Item" of yesterday, July 5. Please charge this purchase to my account.

One phone is to be shipped to me at my address, above,

and the other to 415 Hinman Place, Mamaroneck, NY 10543.

I shall especially appreciate your usual prompt delivery.

Very truly yours,
Julie O'Shea

LETTERS CONFIRMING ORDERS

1.

HarperCollins Publishers
10 East 53rd Street
New York, NY 10022

Dear Sir or Madame:

This letter will confirm my order, placed by telephone this afternoon with your Mr. Arnold, for the following books of your *College Outline Series:*

2 Ancient History @ $17.00	34.00
1 Business Law @ 15.00	15.00
3 French Grammar @ 7.00	21.00
1 Latin America in Maps @ $21.00	21.00
1 Spanish Grammar @ 7.00	7.00
	Total 98.00

Enclosed is my check for the full amount ($98.00). I will appreciate your expediting the order.

Sincerely,
Edward Summers
Purchasing Agent

2.

Dear Circulation Department Manager:

This letter will confirm my order, given in person, to Charles Boswell yesterday afternoon, for yearly subscriptions to the following magazines:

Everybody's World $16.00
Science for You 14.00
Dental Facts 11.00
The World In Brief 22.00
Total $63.00

The magazines are to be sent monthly to my office address, given on this letterhead, but please send acknowledgment and bill to:

Dr. Paul Winslow
414 Wedgemore Road
Leonia, New Jersey 07605

LETTERS ACKNOWLEDGING ORDERS

1.

Dear Mr. Carroll:

We acknowledge with thanks your check and order of November 9 for two extension ladders of the type described in our letter to you of November 2.

It is very unfortunate that the demand has been so great that we have no more of these ladders on hand at present.

We regret, too, that we cannot say just when we shall receive a new supply, which was ordered several days ago.

If you wish, we will gladly return your check and will inform you when the new supply arrives. If, however, you prefer, we will keep your check and forward the ladders to you immediately upon their arrival.

> Sincerely,
> Helmut Brewer

2.

Dear Mr. Caldwell:

Please accept my personal thanks for your order of March 3. It was a pleasure to receive it and to attend to it myself. The merchandise has already been packed, shipped, and is well on its way. You should receive it within twenty-four hours.

I want to add that, while this is the first order you have placed with us, I trust that there will be many more. Let me assure you that we shall spare no effort to justify the confidence you have shown in us and in our product. We take pride in the fact that we have a long list of customers whose first orders were the beginning of a fine business relation ship that still continues.

> Sincerely yours,
> Lillian Woodruff

3.

Dear Mr. Barnes:

Thank you, again, very much, for your purchase of our refrigerator. I did thank you when you gave the order yesterday, at our agency, but I want to express my appreciation once more.

You told me, at that time, that neighbors of yours had recommended us and our merchandise, and that is good to hear, for, after all, other satisfied customers are the best testimony to the quality of our products and our service. We want you to know that we shall not be satisfied until you are satisfied, absolutely, that our refrigerator is really all we say it is.

We stand ready to do any servicing or adjustment, at any time, that may help to give you the 100 percent efficiency that is associated with our products. It will be a pleasure to serve you.

> Very sincerely yours,
> Coleen Seaver

INQUIRY LETTER CONCERNING ORDER

Dear Ms Southport:

Two days ago we received from you a Panorama VCR but there was no letter accompanying it, and none has as yet arrived.

We have referred to our correspondence files, but find nothing from you concerning this matter. In the meantime, our service and repair department has examined your VCR and found that the replacement of two heads is necessary. We assume that you returned the set for this attention, and we are proceeding accordingly.

You will receive the VCR within two days.

> Very truly yours,
> Thomas Spelman

LETTER REGARDING REMITTANCES

Letter Questioning Report of Payment

Dear Gentlemen or Mesdames:

We regret troubling you concerning the matter of payment of our bill for the amount of $225.50 (Invoice No. B 345-829). In your letter of August 2, you state that you had mailed your check, but we have not as yet received it.

Will you please find out whether your bank has cleared it. If it has not, we shall appreciate your sending us a duplicate.

Yours very truly,
Marcia Peyton

Letter Acknowledging Remittance

Dear Mr. Bauer:

Thank you for your check for $35.60 which accompanied your order of July 7. You should receive the merchandise within twenty-four hours, as we have already shipped your order.

We are taking the liberty of enclosing a special announcement of a discount sale, to be held next month, that we are sending now to a selected list of customers.

Sincerely yours,
Angela Kelleher

COLLECTION LETTERS

Good, successful collection letters are of great importance in business, from two standpoints: (1) They bring in money that might have had to be written off the books, or else collected only through litigation. (2) Strange as it may sound, they can actually create good will at the same time that they are persuading debtors to settle delinquent accounts.

But to be successful, collection letters must show patience, tact, and understanding, often in circumstances that are very trying from the collector's standpoint. At the same time, there must be an underlying firmness, which, in the last resort, is converted into the necessary legal action. Certainly, if the collector follows the preliminary path of patience, forbearance, and tact, the debtor can make no just charge of unfairness if the creditor has to take that final step of litigation.

DIRECT REMINDERS OF ACCOUNTS DUE

1.

Dear Mrs. Turner:

Of course, you have many things to remember besides your account with us. We realize that, but one of the things you have forgotten is your check for $75.00, due three months ago.

Since we have our accounts to balance and want to do it without further delay, we are enclosing a stamped, addressed envelope to make it easy for you to send your check by return mail. If this is not possible, will you please inform us when we may expect payment.

Yours very truly,
Walter Stewart

2.

Dear Mr. Churchill:

We believe that you are among the considerable number of our customers who not only do not resent a reminder of an overdue account, but who actually appreciate it. There are so many important matters pressing for attention these days that it is very easy temporarily to overlook a financial obligation.

You will, we are sure, therefore understand the spirit in which this letter is written and will let us have your check at your early convenience. It may even be that you have already mailed it.

If so, thank you, and just forget this letter.

Sincerely,
George A. Halsey

3.

Dear Friendways Customer:

Sending out statements and writing our good customers for money is one thing we do not like to do. We like to see your orders. We like to sell you books. We like to give you service—but we don't like the collecting end of the business.

However, it takes money to run a business, and this business is one that depends on turnover—buying and selling. No matter how badly any salesperson calling on us wants to sell his product, he has to listen to the credit manager for authority and, if we did not pay our bills promptly, we wouldn't be able to have stock for you.

The only reason you are getting this letter is that we believe you have overlooked your account. The amount is $100.24, as shown on the enclosed statement. We hope to receive your check by return mail. Thanks.

Very cordially yours,
Friendways, Inc.

4.

Dear Mr. Wells:

This is a friendly request. It is sent because we believe you have overlooked our invoices of July and August in the amount of $65.35, now just a bit past due.

In view of the possibility that the original invoices were lost, we are enclosing duplicate copies in order that you may see exactly what this amount covers. Knowing full well how busy you are, we send this letter merely as a reminder. We are enclosing a business reply envelope for your convenience in remitting.

Thank you in advance for giving this matter your prompt attention.

Cordially yours,
Radford & Phelps, Inc.

5.

Dear Ms Solomon:

Hold it!

Don't file me in that handsome wastebasket beside your desk. It's crowded, and I don't like crowds.

Not under that pile of mail on your desk, either. I couldn't breathe—and I like to breathe and keep active.

What else do I like?

I like checks, and I like paper clips, and I like action. So just make out a check, fasten it to me with a paper clip, and mail us, right now, to Frierneder Associates.

Always cordially,
Collection Department
Frierneder Associates

6.

Dear Mr. Ford:

In looking over our records, we find that your account shows an unpaid balance totalling $167.91.

We are fully aware that a matter like this slips one's mind. It has happened to us, too. But you must realize that, from our point of view, it is more serious, and we are sure that you understand this. According to our checkup, there is no error in our records, but, if you think there is an error, please let us know.

It will be highly appreciated if you will pay this balance promptly or inform us of any reason why you should not do so.

Yours very truly,
William Farrington

7.

Dear Mr. Devoe:

We felt certain that you would give prompt attention to our recent friendly request for immediate settlement of your unpaid balance of $150.98. It is therefore all the more disappointing that you have not given our reminders the attention they surely deserve.

You have generally paid your obligations promptly, and that is why it seems to us that there must be some good reason why, this time, you have for so long left your balance unpaid. To be exact, it is four months since we first billed you. Don't you think that at least a reasonable explanation is due us? This letter is a sincere and friendly request that you settle the account now.

If you do that, an explanation will not be necessary.

Very truly yours,
Ellery Powell

8.

Dear Ms Foote:

Maybe you just forgot—Or maybe you overlooked it—In either event, the result is the same, so far as we are concerned. We are still looking for the $42.33 that is due monthly as your share in the Fowler Development Project, and in accordance with the contract that you signed.

Twice before we have had to request that you meet this obligation, and we fail to understand why. Please write by return mail and explain—or, much better, send a check for the amount in full.

Yours truly,
Allen B. Fowler

SPECIAL APPEALS AND APPROACHES

Appeal to Customer's Pride

Dear Mr. Nelson:

We are going to be frank and tell you something that we believe you would like to know.

We have recently had correspondence with another large firm, asking us specifically about your credit standing with us. Until very recently, we could have told them that you were among our best and most valued customers in the matter of paying your bills promptly and in full. But now, your May account is still unsettled, after five months, and in spite of several requests from us. You take pride, we are sure, in your business reputation, and we are equally certain that this neglect of yours is a careless oversight. There is still time to remedy the matter if you will send us a remittance by return mail.

In that case, we can still recommend you to the firm in question, for we honestly believe that in the future you will be careful to live up to the excellent reputation that you had established with us.

Yours very truly,
Arthur Moss

Appeal to Customer's Fairness

Dear Mr. Paddock:

If we should happen to meet you on the street and pass the time of day with you, we are certain that you not only would think of that unpaid balance of yours ($156.23), but would mention it.

More than that, we believe that you would give us some good reason why you have not settled your account with us.

You won't think us unfair, we are sure, if we ask you to write a little note, now, and explain why you have neglected this matter—or, better still, enclose a check with your note.

We believe you will agree that we have been fair in this matter.

Now won't you be fair with us?

Very truly yours,
Hudson Valley Company, Inc.

Appeal to Customer's Understanding

Dear Accounts Payable Director:

You know, and we know, that good business is built on mutual understanding—one person's appreciating the other person's point of view.

We appreciated your point of view three months ago, when we took special pains to attend promptly to your order. Twice we have requested payment, but with no result —not even a reply. You realize, we are sure, that it is prompt remittances that make it possible to continue serving you and other good customers. We are sure, too, that you would have been very much put out if we had neglected your order the way you have neglected payment.

Won't you send us immediately a check for the enclosed duplicate statement?

Yours truly,
Melissa Cohen

Appeal to Customer's Self-Interest

Dear Mrs. Brandon:

First of all, we want you to know that we consider you a good customer, even though you have owed us payment of $45 for three months now.

Not very many customers realize that it is to their own best interest to pay their bills regularly and promptly, but it is. Therefore it is not just for our own sake that we are urging you to clear this account now. If we are to maintain our standards of quality and fair prices, we must have the cash to pay our own bills promptly, and we cannot do that unless our customers do the same by us. So you see that we

have your welfare in mind when we asked you for a check
by return mail.

We look forward to your continued patronage.

Yours very truly,
Addison Williams

P.S. The enclosed "preview" of our February sale may interest you.

Letter with Humorous Angle

Dear Customer:

We had thought of having some mourning stationery
printed for writing to people like you, with accounts long
overdue. Then we thought better of it, for we didn't want
to make you feel as sad about it as we do.

It always makes us feel especially sad when we find new
names among our monthly past-due accounts. This month,
your name was there, as large as life. There is, however, a
bright part to the story—this is the first time you have
appeared on the list, and we congratulate you on that.

We're sure it was all a mistake—on your part—and that
you'll never let it happen again. So just rush a check by
return mail, and all will be forgiven.

Cordially,
Adam Zabriskie

LETTERS REGARDING A TIME EXTENSION

Request for a Time Extension

Dear Ms Switzer:

I am answering promptly your letter of yesterday, urging me to settle my account, now three months overdue, for I want you to know that I am sincere and have no desire to disregard my obligations.

In reply to a similar letter of yours, two weeks ago, I explained that I was having some financial difficulties, and asked that you bear with me a little longer. You know that until recently my credit with you was excellent, and this fact should convince you that I am not now trying to evade my just debts. Certainly such is not the case.

I did not go into details before, because I presumed that my statement about financial troubles would be satisfactory to you. But now let me tell you that within the period in question both my wife and I have been ill, and that my wife's case has required very considerable medical expense and hospitalization. Moreover, since my work is on a straight commission basis, and I was ill for some time, my income was seriously depleted.

Now I am back at work, but I cannot very soon recoup my losses, particularly since my wife is still under a physician's care.

I feel sure you will understand my explanation, which is given in all good faith and without exaggeration. I should be glad to refer you to our physician for corroboration of my statements. I merely ask that you grant me a little more time and I will fully meet all my obligations.

> Yours very truly,
> Winthrop D. Heatley

Grant of Time Extension

Dear Mr. Heatley:

We appreciate your letter giving a detailed explanation of your failure for so long to settle your account. If you had written this letter a good many weeks ago, you would have spared both yourself and us a good deal of unnecessary anxiety and unpleasantness.

Sometimes, in cases like this, a customer looks upon a business organization as a mere machine with no sympathy or understanding. If that was your idea, we are going to prove right now that you were wrong. We accept your explanation, and we are sorry to hear about all the illness and expense you and your wife have had to face.

Even in instances like this, however, we do not always make the concession we are going to make to you. But you have had a good record with us, and we have faith in your sincerity and integrity. Therefore, we are granting you an extension of sixty days from today's date, without even requiring that you sign a note.

We sincerely hope that all will be well with you in the very near future.

> Very truly yours,
> Robert Southers

SERIES OF COLLECTION LETTERS
AND FOLLOW-UPS

1.

Dear Mr. Clement:

It may be that our recent request for settlement of your overdue account of $198.45 was mislaid for some reason or other. Generally you have been prompt in your payments.

We shall appreciate your giving this matter your immediate attention. Enclosed is an itemized statement, for your convenience.

Very truly yours,
Robert Nichols

Enclosure

2.

Dear Mr. Clement:

We regret the necessity of again reminding you of your unpaid bill of $198.45, now six months overdue.

In our letter of two weeks ago, we enclosed an itemized statement for you to check. Since we have received no letter taking exception, we assume that the bill is correct.

Kindly send us remittance immediately, or explain any further delay.

Yours very truly,
Robert Nichols

3.

Dear Mr. Clement:

In spite of our having recently reminded you twice of
your delinquent account with us, we are still willing to
assume that your case may be one of overlooking, rather
than of disregarding, our requests.

You can easily prove our assumption correct by sending
us at once, in the enclosed return envelope, your check for
the amount in full that you owe.

Won't you act now?

> Yours very truly,
> Robert Nichols

4.

Dear Mr. Clement:

It is unpleasant, exasperating, and expensive to continue
carrying your long-overdue account on our books, and to
have to write letter after letter requesting you to pay the
$198.45 that you still owe us. We have not even received
the courtesy of a reply.

Therefore, we have regretfully reached the conclusion
that there is left only the final resort to legal measures, and
we have placed your case in the hands of our attorney.

> Yours very truly,
> Robert Nichols

Letter from Attorney to Customer

Dear Mr. Clement:

This morning I received from Mr. Robert Nichols full information regarding your delinquent account with his firm, together with a letter authorizing me to collect the amount ($198.45) now long overdue.

You have neither denied the claim nor given Mr. Nichols any explanation of your failure to meet your obligation. Therefore, I hereby notify you that, unless I hear from you within seven days, I will institute legal proceedings for the collection of the sum herein mentioned.

Very truly yours,
Arthur B. Vandeventer
Attorney-at-Law

Letter from Customer to Attorney

Dear Mr. Vandeventer:

I have your letter threatening legal action to collect my overdue account of $198.45 with Mr. Nichols' firm.

There is no question as to the claim. Moreover, I have doubtless been very foolish to disregard Mr. Nichols' numerous communications, but I have had the perhaps mistaken idea that, in the circumstances, nothing would have been gained by writing.

Now, however, let me explain that, within the period in question, my business failed and I have had an extremely difficult time settling my affairs, and also forming a new connection. This I have finally succeeded in doing, and the outlook is good.

Tomorrow I will drop in at your office and will make

payment of at least one-third of the amount I owe. The balance I believe I can settle in the near future.

I trust that this arrangement will be satisfactory to you and Mr. Nichols, and I am sorry for the inconvenience that I have caused.

Sincerely yours,
Ward B. Clement

CREDIT LETTERS

Too often, the underlying meaning of the word credit is forgotten. Derived from the Latin, it means "faith," or "confidence." Credit is the foundation of business on the highest plane. Those who write credit letters would do well to remember the fundamental meaning of the word. The person who requests credit should expect to furnish a basis for confidence upon which the creditor can establish a satisfactory relationship.

The credit agent should write letters that are dignified, straightforward, sincere—letters that make it clear that the interests of the prospective customer and of the firm are the same. Even a letter refusing credit, or suspending it, if skillfully written, can carry with it a spirit of good will that may yet be the means of establishing a mutually successful and pleasant business relationship.

REQUESTS FOR CREDIT

An Order Accompanied by Request for Credit

Dear Order Manager:

I should like to order two dozen pairs of your men's shoes No. 4621 A at $30.50 a pair, as listed in your April retailer catalog.

Also, I request that you open an account for my store with the order listed above. The following references will furnish, I am sure, all the desired information and recommendations as to my business standing that you may require:

> Brown, Carroll & Co.
> 106 Waltham Street
> West Newton, MA 02165
>
> Saunders & Emory
> 111 Oaklawn Avenue
> Cranston, Rhode Island 02920

As I wish to push my spring business, I shall sincerely appreciate your establishing my credit account at your earliest possible convenience.

> Yours truly,
> John Giroux

Request for Opening of Account

Dear Sir or Madam:

This is to request that I be allowed to open a credit account with your organization.

No doubt, you will recall that I have been buying auto parts from you for some time now, on a C.O.D. basis, but I should like the decided convenience of charging my purchases. What I want is an arrangement whereby I can pay my bills within thirty days from the date I receive my invoice.

My business has grown materially during the past year, and I have recently added to my lists such substantial customers as Swiftway Trucking Company, Morrison Storage & Van Company, and the Hillcrest Garage and Servicing Chain.

I have my account in Hillcrest Bank and Trust Company and gladly refer you to their vice president, Ms Samantha Rune. Other references who will vouch for my personal and business integrity and reliability are:

> Wentworth Auto Supply Corporation
> 13 Westridge Drive
> Simsbury, CT 06070
>
> Ainsley & Son
> 1122 Skyline
> Neosha, MO 64850
>
> Powers & Aimes
> 1905 Highland View Avenue
> Powell, OH 43065

I am certain that the references given herewith will prove entirely satisfactory, and I therefore hope to hear favorably from you in the very near future.

> Yours truly,
> Ellsworth Morrow

Inquiries Regarding Credit Standing, and Replies

1.

Dear Sir or Madam:

William A. Arnold, Inc., recently gave us your name as a reference when they applied for a credit account with us.

Will you kindly furnish us with all pertinent information regarding the firm in question, particularly as regards the promptness and regularity with which they meet their financial obligations. Of course, anything you tell us will be treated entirely confidentially.

As we should like to inform the Arnold company at the earliest opportunity, we shall sincerely appreciate hearing from you soon. We shall be glad to do you a similar favor at any time.

Sincerely,
Mark H. Coleman

2.

Dear Mr. Lovejoy:

We have received from Mr. James A. Gable, of 42 Cowan Boulevard, Symington, Kentucky, a request that we grant him a line of credit, and your name is among the references that he has given.

It will be highly appreciated if you will send us, in the enclosed return envelope, a perfectly frank statement concerning his dealings with you, and your opinion as to his character, integrity, and financial dependability.

You may be sure that this report will be treated as strictly confidential. Thank you for your valuable cooperation.

Very truly yours,

James B. Welch

Reply to Letter #1.

Dear Mr. Coleman:

As requested, we are replying with perfect frankness to your recent letter of inquiry regarding William A. Arnold, Inc., as a credit risk.

We regret having to tell you that, in all fairness to you, we cannot recommend the firm. Although for six months we did grant them generous credit privileges, they proved remiss in their payments and disregarded our appeals that they meet their obligations as agreed. Consequently, we were obliged to withdraw those privileges and do business with them only on a strictly cash basis.

That is the only basis we consider safe for dealing with the firm in question.

Yours truly,

Robert Mead

Reply to Letter #2.

Dear Mr. Welch:

It is a pleasure to answer your letter asking about Mr. James A. Gable.

We have dealt with Mr. Gable for four years—on a credit basis all that time—and consider ourselves fortunate to have him as a customer. He has never had a past-due account. Not only that, but he has sent us quite a few customers equally reliable. Evidently, to judge from his purchases, his business is highly successful.

We recommend him to you with no reservations.

Yours very truly,
Frederick B. Lovejoy

REPLIES TO CUSTOMERS WHO HAVE REQUESTED CREDIT

Letter Granting Credit

Dear Mr. Ward:

Thank you for the expression of confidence and good will that your request for a charge account implies.

The references you submitted have been checked, and we compliment you on the high esteem in which you are held by those with whom you deal. An account has been opened for you and we trust that you will make use of it soon, and often. You will find ordering by telephone a convenience, and such orders will receive prompt and courteous attention.

We send our statements the last of each month, and we shall appreciate payment sometime within the month immediately following.

Advance notice of special sales and other features of interest will be sent you as a credit customer, and we shall spare no effort to make all your dealings with us pleasant and satisfactory.

Sincerely yours,
James Ettinger

Letter Refusing Credit

Gentlemen or Mesdames:

First of all, thank you for your large order for Pure-Air Ventilators, which you placed with our Mr. Thatcher on March 4, and your request that we open a credit account for your firm.

We are sure you understand that, before we authorize such an account, we try to get all possible information that might justify our granting a line of credit. This we have done in your case. Please do not misunderstand, but on the basis of facts and figures so far secured, we have not been able to make a definite decision to grant you the credit requested.

In view of the circumstances, we do not at present feel quite justified in opening an account for you. If you think that our decision is unwarranted, or if you can furnish us with information that we now lack, do not hesitate to write us or call personally at our office. We should be most happy to reach a better understanding.

It may well be that circumstances may change and that we might then be able to accede to your request. In the meantime, we do value your patronage and shall be happy to serve you, as before, on a C.O.D. basis.

Very truly yours,
William T. Ainslee

Letter Notifying of Credit Suspension

Dear Sir or Madam:

We wish to thank you for your generous order received yesterday, which you asked us to ship immediately and charge to your account.

Your order is already being assembled. However, you probably have overlooked the fact that for some months you have allowed your account to go unsettled. Since it is our policy to suspend credit until all past-due bills are paid, we request that you send us immediate remittance for the statement already twice rendered. You will understand that no discrimination against you is intended or implied.

Our only wish is to serve you promptly, and we will ship your order immediately upon receipt of your check.

Yours sincerely,

Richard Hammond

GOOD-WILL LETTERS

Most business letters can, and should, be good-will letters—yes, even those dealing with collection and refusal of credit. It is the spirit, not the subject matter, that counts.

The correspondence in this section is designed to illustrate the type written primarily to build good will, without which no business can long exist. This kind should be relatively informal and entirely sincere. It should not indicate or imply that it is a lure to get or keep customers. It should reflect a genuine friendliness that will prove to the recipient that not all dealings are "strictly business." Such letters pay generous dividends.

The following examples illustrate sound underlying principles.

Welcome to a New Customer

Dear Miss Ray:

This is a friendly note of welcome as you become a depositor in The People's Bank.

Too often business is done on a purely formal and impersonal basis, but we don't subscribe to that policy. We try to live up to the title of our institution, and we want you to think of us not merely as cashiers, tellers, and bank officials, but as friends of yours—all of us—who stand ready to serve you in every possible way.

We shall be happy to give you the benefit of our long and thorough experience in financial matters, at any time, and we feel sure this is the beginning of a long and pleasant relationship.

> Cordially yours,
> Anna Lee Chang
> President

Keeping the Product Sold

Dear Mr. Rodriguez:

Three weeks ago, we sold you one of our Wellbilt power mowers, and we feel sure that it is proving to be all that it is claimed to be.

But we should be very glad to hear from you anyway, because it is always a pleasure to receive word from customers who are entirely satisfied with our products. Indeed, that is the biggest satisfaction in business.

We want to emphasize again that we shall be happy to make any adjustments of the machine, at any time, that will insure its operation at top performance.

Thank you again for your patronage.

Sincerely yours,

Donald Blaine

APPROACHING A PROSPECTIVE CUSTOMER

Dear Mrs. Wainwright:

May we bid you a sincere welcome as a new resident of Great Falls?

We are certain that you are going to like this community, and that you will find the business people just as much friends of yours as the neighbors who live on your block.

When you are downtown, shopping, won't you make Easton's Restaurant a regular stopping place for lunch? You will find here not only delicious food at moderate prices, but quick, efficient service and a restful, homey atmosphere that will make every call a real pleasure.

I shall look forward to welcoming you personally, and soon, I hope.

Cordially yours,

Mary E. Bull

Manager

HOLIDAY GREETING

Dear Mr. Collingwell:

It is good, at least once a year, to lay aside business formalities and to write a letter purely in the spirit of the season.

You have long been a very good customer, but, more than that, you are also a very good friend, and I want you to know that I truly value that relationship. If you never gave me another order, I would still want you as a friend. I just wouldn't feel right if you weren't dropping in every little while.

So here are my warmest and most sincere holiday greetings to you and yours. May all the true happiness of the season be yours, and may it continue with you throughout the coming year.

Sincerely,
Anton B. Drew

INDEX

ABOUT THE AUTHOR

The late ALFRED STUART MYERS was an experienced writer and editor, formerly head of the English Department at Idaho Industrial Institute and instructor in English at Maryville College. He contributed numerous articles to *Advertising and Selling*, *Industrial Management*, *Printer's Ink*, *The Writer*, and other national journals. During World War II he was in charge of correspondence in one of the largest government branches of the Office of Dependency Benefits. For many years he served as a freelance editor for leading book publishers and edited notable works in advertising, business management, economics, engineering, history, medicine, and sociology. *Letters for All Occasions* has continued to be a best-selling reference, a tribute to Mr. Myers' foresight forty years ago when it was first published.

LYNN FERRARI, while preserving the flavor, charm, and unique formality of Mr. Myers' original book, has revised and updated each chapter to reflect the changes in lifestyle and technology that have taken place through the decades. Although invitations for yachting weekends and bridge luncheons are still included, letters from women corporate presidents and guidelines for communications via fax and electronic computer mail have been added—types of correspondence unheard of when Mr. Myers initially wrote this book!

Ms Ferrari, former executive editor of Vogue Patterns publications, has an extensive background in publishing, advertising, and communications. She has served as editor and writer for a number of other HarperCollins books, as etiquette editor for *Millionaire Magazine*, and as contributing editor for *Bridal Guide Magazine*. Her freelance career also includes the publication of articles on a wide range of topics for many other national periodicals and the coordination of marketing, advertising, communications, and public information programs for a variety of organizations, businesses, and institutions.

■ HarperPaperbacks

Have all the information you need at your fingertips with these handy reference guides!

❏ **American Slang** 109284-3 ....$5.99

❏ **Spell It Right!** 100814-1 ....$4.99

❏ **Punctuate It Right!** 100813-3 ....$4.99

❏ **Errors in English and Ways to Correct Them** 100815-X............$4.99

❏ **Speed Reading** 109301-7 ....$4.99

❏ **Writing That Works** 109381-5 ....$4.99

❏ **The Concise Roget's International Thesaurus** 100709-9 ....$4.99

❏ **Letters for All Occasions** 109283-5 ....$5.99

❏ **The Resume Writer's Handbook** 109300-9 ....$4.99

❏ **The Crossword Puzzle Dictionary** 100038-8 ....$5.99

❏ **Revised Funk & Wagnalls Standard Dictionary** 100708-0 ......$4.99

❏ **Collins French-English Dictionary** 100244-5..........................$4.99

❏ **Collins German-English Dictionary** 100243-7 ....$4.99

❏ **Collins Italian-English Dictionary** 100246-1 ....$4.99

❏ **Collins Spanish-English Dictionary** 100245-3 ....$4.99

*Add $1.00 per title to U.S. price for sales in Canada.

MAIL TO: **HarperCollins Publishers**
          P.O. Box 588 Dunmore, PA 18512-0588
          OR CALL: **(800) 331-3761 (Visa/Mastercard)**
Yes, please send me the books I have checked:

SUBTOTAL ....$_____

POSTAGE AND HANDLING . ...$ 2.00_____

SALES TAX (Add applicable sales tax) ....$_____

Name_____

Address_____

City_____

State_____Zip_____

*Order 4 or more titles and postage and handling is free! Order less than 4 books, please include $2.00 postage & handling. Remit in U.S. funds. Do not send cash.

Allow up to 6 weeks for delivery. (Valid in U.S. & Canada.)
Prices subject to change.   HO961